Beyond Authority- Unleashing The True Power Of Leadership

Adam Poliman

Published by Adam Poliman, 2023.

While every precaution has been taken in the preparation of this book, the publisher assumes no responsibility for errors or omissions, or for damages resulting from the use of the information contained herein.

BEYOND AUTHORITY- UNLEASHING THE TRUE POWER OF LEADERSHIP

First edition. August 24, 2023.

ISBN: 979-8215971086

Written by Adam Poliman.

Also by Adam Poliman

Watch for more at https://optimizationtime.com.

Are you tired of feeling limited by your position of authority? Do you long to unleash the true power of your leadership?

Look no further, because in this book, we will take you on a journey beyond authority, where you will discover the key to unlocking your full leadership potential.

In the world of leadership, it's not just about having a title or being in charge. True leadership goes beyond authority and is about inspiring, motivating, and guiding others towards a common goal. It's about having the ability to influence and make a positive impact, regardless of your position.

In this book, we will explore the different dimensions of leadership, from defining what it truly means to be a leader, to understanding the various leadership styles and theories. We will delve into the importance of emotional intelligence and ethics in leadership, as well as the intricate relationship between power and leadership.

Additionally, we will provide practical tips for cultivating future leaders and evaluating and developing your own leadership skills.

So get ready to go beyond authority and tap into the true power of leadership.

Chapter 1: Defining Leadership

When exploring the subtopic of leadership, it's important to understand the nature of leadership itself.

As a leader, your role holds great influence, as you have the power to inspire and guide others towards a common goal.

Good leadership isn't simply about authority, but about tapping into the true essence of leadership, which lies in your ability to communicate effectively and connect with those you lead.

The Nature of Leadership

If you're looking to understand the true nature of leadership and go beyond the traditional idea of authority, then this discussion is for you.

We'll explore what leadership really means and delve into the key attributes that make a great leader.

Additionally, we'll distinguish between leadership and management, highlighting the unique qualities that set them apart.

By the end of this discussion, you'll have a clearer understanding of the power and potential of true leadership.

What Is Leadership?

Leadership, at its core, is about inspiring and empowering others to reach their full potential.

It isn't just about giving orders or being in a position of authority, but about creating a vision and guiding others towards it.

True leaders understand the importance of collaboration and teamwork, and they know how to motivate and mobilize their team members towards a common goal.

They're able to communicate effectively, listen actively, and provide guidance and support when needed.

Leadership isn't about being the smartest or most talented person in the room, but about bringing out the best in others and creating an environment where everyone can thrive.

It's about leading by example, setting high standards, and encouraging innovation and creativity.

In essence, leadership is about making a positive impact on the lives of others and leaving a lasting legacy.

Attributes of Leadership

Leadership is about inspiring and empowering others to reach their full potential, creating a vision and guiding others towards it, and fostering collaboration and teamwork.

As a leader, you must possess certain attributes that enable you to effectively lead and influence others.

One important attribute is self-confidence, which allows you to believe in yourself and your abilities, inspiring others to have confidence in you as well.

Additionally, strong communication skills are essential for effectively conveying your vision and goals to your team, as well as for listening and providing feedback.

Another crucial attribute is empathy, as being able to understand and connect with others on an emotional level fosters trust and loyalty.

Finally, adaptability and resilience are key qualities that enable you to navigate through challenges and setbacks, demonstrating to others that you can handle adversity and inspire them to do the same.

By embodying these attributes, you can unleash the true power of leadership and create a positive and productive work environment.

Leadership vs. Management

When it comes to leading a team, you need to understand the difference between being a leader and being a manager, so you can effectively guide and motivate your team towards success.

While management focuses on tasks, processes, and maintaining order, leadership is about inspiring and influencing others to achieve a common goal.

Managers often rely on their formal authority, whereas leaders inspire trust and respect through their actions and character.

A leader understands the strengths and weaknesses of their team members and knows how to leverage those strengths to maximize performance.

They empower their team by providing guidance and support, fostering an environment of collaboration and growth.

A leader motivates their team by setting clear goals, providing meaningful feedback, and recognizing achievements.

By understanding the distinction between leadership and management, you can unlock the true power of leadership and create a high-performing team that is driven to achieve extraordinary results.

The Influential Role of Leaders

In this discussion, you'll explore the influential role that leaders play in their organizations.

You'll gain an understanding of how leaders can effectively use their influence to inspire and motivate their teams.

Additionally, you'll learn practical strategies for gaining influence and putting it into action to achieve your goals as a leader.

Understanding Influence

Explore the depths of your own influence and how it can shape the world around you. Influence is a powerful tool that every leader possesses, regardless of their position or authority.

It is not solely dependent on the title you hold or the number of people you manage; rather, it is about the impact you have on others and the ability to inspire and motivate them towards a common goal. Understanding influence means recognizing that it goes beyond the traditional notion of power and control.

It is about building relationships, earning trust, and leveraging your unique strengths to bring about positive change. By harnessing your influence, you can create a ripple effect that extends far beyond your immediate sphere of influence, touching the lives of those around you and even shaping the future.

So, take a moment to reflect on the power of your influence and how you can use it to make a difference in the world.

Gaining Influence

Gaining influence is all about building genuine connections and using your unique strengths to make a lasting impact on others, lighting a fire within them that spreads like wildfire.

It's not about wielding power or authority, but rather about understanding and connecting with people on a deeper level.

To gain influence, you need to be authentic and true to yourself, allowing others to see your genuine passion and commitment. By leveraging your strengths, whether it's your expertise, charisma, or ability to inspire, you can inspire others to follow your lead.

Building trust is crucial in gaining influence, as people are more likely to listen and be influenced by someone they trust. This means being reliable, transparent, and consistent in your actions and words.

Additionally, being a good listener and genuinely caring about others' perspectives and needs can go a long way in building influence. By empathizing with others and addressing their concerns, you show that you value their input and are willing to work collaboratively towards a common goal.

Ultimately, gaining influence is about creating a positive impact in the lives of others, empowering them to reach their full potential and achieve success.

Influence In Action

Take a moment to witness the incredible impact that influence can have when it's put into action.

When you harness your influence and use it effectively, you have the power to inspire, motivate, and guide others towards a common goal.

Influence in action is about leading by example, showing empathy, and building trust.

It's about using your words and actions to create a positive and supportive environment where people feel empowered and valued.

By leading with influence, you can bring out the best in others, encourage collaboration, and foster innovation.

So, take the opportunity to leverage your influence and make a real difference in the lives of those around you.

The Essence of Good Leadership

When it comes to good leadership, vision is crucial. Having a clear and compelling vision not only inspires others, but it also provides a sense of direction and purpose.

Initiative is another key aspect of good leadership, as it involves taking proactive steps to bring that vision to life.

Empathy is equally important, as it allows leaders to understand and connect with their team members on a deeper level, fostering trust and collaboration.

Lastly, persistence is essential in overcoming challenges and setbacks, as it demonstrates resilience and determination.

By embodying these qualities, you can unleash the true power of leadership and guide your team towards success.

Vision

Imagine a world where leaders have the power to inspire and guide others towards a shared vision, creating a future that surpasses all expectations.

Vision is the cornerstone of effective leadership, as it provides a clear direction and purpose for the team. A leader with a compelling vision can motivate their followers to go above and beyond, to overcome obstacles and achieve greatness.

A strong vision not only gives meaning to the work being done, but it also provides a roadmap for success. It allows leaders to set goals, make decisions, and allocate resources in a way that aligns with their desired future.

Without vision, leadership becomes aimless and ineffective, lacking the ability to inspire and mobilize others towards a common goal.

As a leader, it's important to cultivate a clear and compelling vision, one that resonates with your team and ignites their passion.

Communicate this vision with enthusiasm and conviction, painting a vivid picture of the future you want to create.

By doing so, you'll unleash the true power of leadership and unlock the potential within your team to achieve remarkable things.

Initiative

Seize the opportunity and show some gumption by taking the initiative to lead others towards a shared vision of success. Initiative is the driving force behind effective leadership, as it requires a proactive mindset and a willingness to take action.

When you take the initiative, you demonstrate your commitment to the vision and inspire others to do the same. By being proactive and taking charge, you create a sense of ownership and empowerment within your team.

Initiative also allows you to anticipate and address potential challenges before they arise, fostering a culture of problem-solving and innovation. As a leader, it's crucial to encourage and empower your team members to take initiative, as it not only leads to greater productivity and success but also cultivates a sense of ownership and pride in their work.

So, don't wait for permission or direction - take the initiative and lead others towards a shared vision of success.

Empathy

Understanding and connecting with others' emotions is a key aspect of effective leadership. Empathy allows you to build strong relationships and create a supportive and inclusive work environment. When you empathize with your team members, you're able to put yourself in their shoes and understand their perspectives, feelings, and challenges.

This not only helps you better understand their needs and motivations but also enables you to provide the necessary support and guidance. By actively listening and showing genuine concern, you can create an environment where people feel valued, heard, and understood. This, in turn, fosters trust and loyalty among your team members, enhancing collaboration and productivity.

Additionally, empathy helps you anticipate potential conflicts or issues before they arise, allowing you to address them proactively. By demonstrating empathy, you can inspire and motivate your team, leading to increased engagement and a sense of belonging.

Ultimately, being empathetic as a leader enables you to create a positive and inclusive work culture that drives success and employee satisfaction.

Persistence

Don't give up, even when faced with challenges that seem insurmountable, because persistence is the key to achieving your goals and overcoming obstacles.

Persistence is the unwavering determination to keep going, even in the face of setbacks and failures. It is the ability to stay focused on your objective and keep pushing forward, no matter how difficult the journey may be.

When you encounter obstacles along the way, remember that they are not roadblocks, but rather opportunities for growth and learning. Embrace these challenges as stepping stones towards your ultimate success.

Stay committed to your vision and keep taking small steps towards your goals, even when progress seems slow. Remember that success rarely happens overnight, but it is the result of consistent effort and perseverance.

So, don't give up. Keep pushing forward, stay resilient, and you will eventually achieve what you set out to accomplish.

Effective Communication in Leadership

When it comes to effective communication in leadership, there are three key points that you must focus on: non-verbal communication, listening skills, and the art of persuasion.

Non-verbal communication, such as body language and facial expressions, can speak volumes and convey messages that words alone cannot.

Listening skills are crucial for understanding and empathizing with your team members, and the art of persuasion allows you to influence and inspire others to take action.

By mastering these three elements, you can become a more effective and impactful leader.

Non-verbal Communication

Body language can reveal more about your true intentions and feelings than words alone. Non-verbal communication plays a crucial role in leadership, as it can convey confidence, trustworthiness, and credibility.

By paying attention to your body language, you can effectively communicate your message and influence others. Simple gestures like maintaining eye contact, having an open posture, and using appropriate facial expressions can make a significant impact on how your message is received. A firm handshake, for example, can convey confidence and establish a sense of trust. On the other hand, crossed arms or fidgeting can make you appear defensive or disinterested.

Being aware of your non-verbal cues and using them intentionally can enhance your leadership abilities and help you connect with others on a deeper level. So, remember to not only focus on what you say, but also how you say it through your body language.

Listening Skills

Now that you've learned about the importance of non-verbal communication, it's time to shift our focus to another essential aspect of effective leadership: listening skills.

As a leader, it's crucial to not only communicate your thoughts and ideas clearly but also to actively listen to others. Listening goes beyond simply hearing what someone's saying; it involves paying attention to their words, understanding their perspective, and empathizing with their emotions.

By honing your listening skills, you can create a more inclusive and collaborative environment, build stronger relationships, and make better-informed decisions.

So, take the time to truly listen to those around you, ask thoughtful questions, and show genuine interest in their thoughts and opinions. Remember, great leaders aren't just great speakers; they're great listeners too.

Art of Persuasion

The art of persuasion is an essential skill for leaders to master in order to effectively influence and inspire others. By understanding the psychology behind persuasion, leaders can tailor their communication strategies to appeal to the emotions, values, and needs of their audience.

Persuasion is not about manipulating or coercing others, but rather about presenting compelling arguments and ideas that resonate with people on a deeper level. It involves building trust, establishing credibility, and creating a shared vision that motivates and engages others.

Effective persuasion requires active listening, empathy, and the ability to communicate with clarity and conviction. Leaders who excel in the art of persuasion can inspire their teams to exceed expectations, drive change, and achieve remarkable results.

Chapter 2: Leadership Styles

In this chapter, you'll explore three key leadership styles: autocratic, democratic, and transformational.

Autocratic leadership involves making decisions without input from others, giving leaders complete authority.

Democratic leadership, on the other hand, emphasizes collaboration and shared decision-making, allowing team members to have a say in the decision-making process.

Lastly, transformational leadership focuses on inspiring and motivating followers through a visionary approach, encouraging personal growth and development.

Understanding these different leadership styles will help you navigate various leadership situations with insight and practicality.

Autocratic Leadership

When it comes to Autocratic Leadership, there are both pros and cons to consider.

On the positive side, this leadership style allows for quick decision-making and efficient execution of tasks. However, it can also lead to a lack of collaboration and employee dissatisfaction.

To implement Autocratic Leadership effectively, it's crucial to clearly communicate expectations and provide a supportive environment where employees feel heard and valued.

Pro's and Con's of Autocratic Leadership

Imagine yourself standing at the crossroads of leadership, where the iron fist of autocratic leadership can either forge an empire or shatter it into a million pieces.

Autocratic leadership, characterized by a leader who holds absolute power and makes decisions without input from others, has its pros and cons. On the positive side, this style of leadership allows for quick decision-making, as there's no need to consult or consider the opinions of others. It can be effective in times of crisis or when immediate action is required.

Additionally, autocratic leaders are often seen as strong and decisive, instilling a sense of confidence in their followers. However, there are downsides to autocratic leadership as well. By limiting the input and involvement of others, it can stifle creativity and innovation within the team. This top-down approach may also lead to resentment and a lack of motivation among team members, resulting in decreased productivity.

Ultimately, the success of autocratic leadership depends on the specific situation and the individuals involved. It's important for leaders to weigh the benefits and drawbacks carefully and consider alternative leadership styles that may better suit the needs of their team.

Implementation of Autocratic Leadership

Autocratic leadership, with its absolute power and lack of input from others, can be implemented in a way that both commands attention and raises eyebrows.

When implementing autocratic leadership, it's important to establish clear expectations and guidelines for the team members. By setting strict rules and procedures, you can ensure that tasks are completed efficiently and effectively.

Additionally, it's crucial to communicate with your team members in a direct and assertive manner. This will help to establish your authority and ensure that your instructions are followed. However, it's important to strike a balance between being assertive and being overly controlling.

While autocratic leadership can be effective in certain situations, it's important to consider the impact it may have on team morale and motivation. By being mindful of these factors and adapting your approach as needed, you can successfully implement autocratic leadership and achieve desired results.

Democratic Leadership

If you're looking to explore the pros and cons of democratic leadership, there are a few key points to consider.

On the positive side, democratic leadership encourages collaboration and fosters a sense of ownership among team members. However, it can also lead to slower decision-making and potential conflicts due to differing opinions.

When implementing democratic leadership, it's important to strike a balance between empowering team members and ensuring efficient decision-making processes.

Pro's and Con's of Democratic Leadership

You'll find that democratic leadership can be a real rollercoaster ride, with its ups and downs, as everyone has a say, but decisions can take forever to be made.

On one hand, democratic leadership promotes collaboration and inclusivity, allowing all team members to contribute their ideas and opinions. This fosters a sense of ownership and commitment among employees, as they feel valued and heard. Additionally, diverse perspectives can lead to more innovative and creative solutions to problems.

However, the downside of democratic leadership is that it can be time-consuming and inefficient. With everyone having a say, it can be challenging to reach a consensus, resulting in long and drawn-out decision-making processes. This can lead to frustration and delays in implementing necessary changes or taking timely action.

It's important for leaders to strike a balance between inclusivity and efficiency, ensuring that the democratic process doesn't hinder progress and productivity.

Implementation of Democratic Leadership

To effectively implement democratic leadership, you need to embrace the power of collaboration and tap into the collective wisdom of your team. This involves creating a vibrant and dynamic work environment where ideas flourish and decisions are made collectively.

By encouraging open communication and active participation from every member, you can harness the diverse perspectives and expertise within your team. This leads to more innovative solutions and better decision-making.

Encourage your team members to share their ideas and opinions, creating a culture of trust and respect. Actively listen to their input, valuing their contributions and incorporating their feedback into the decision-making process.

Foster a sense of ownership and accountability by involving your team in setting goals and objectives. This empowers them to take ownership of their work.

By implementing democratic leadership, you can create a work environment that not only fosters creativity and collaboration but also promotes a strong sense of teamwork and individual growth.

Transformational Leadership

When considering the pros and cons of transformational leadership, it's important to recognize the potential benefits it can bring to an organization.

Transformational leaders have the ability to inspire and motivate their followers, leading to increased productivity and innovation.

However, there are also potential drawbacks to this leadership style. These include the risk of placing too much power in the hands of one individual and the potential for followers to become overly dependent on the leader.

When implementing transformational leadership, it's crucial to strike a balance between empowering and guiding followers, while also ensuring that there is a system of checks and balances in place to prevent any potential abuses of power.

Pro's and Con's of Transformational Leadership

Despite its benefits in promoting employee motivation and fostering innovation, transformational leadership also carries the risk of creating unrealistic expectations and overdependence on the leader.

When leaders inspire and motivate their team members to reach new heights, it can lead to increased job satisfaction and productivity.

However, this can also create a sense of idealism that may be difficult to sustain in the long run.

Employees may start to expect constant inspiration and guidance from their leader, which can be unrealistic and unsustainable. Moreover, overdependence on the leader can hinder team members' autonomy and creativity, as they may rely too heavily on the leader's direction and approval.

It is important for leaders practicing transformational leadership to strike a balance between inspiring their team and encouraging independence. By setting realistic expectations and empowering their team members to take ownership of their work, leaders can foster a culture of innovation and growth while avoiding the drawbacks of overdependence and unrealistic expectations.

Implementation of Transformational Leadership

The implementation of transformational leadership has been shown to have a significant impact on employee satisfaction. Studies indicate that organizations with transformational leaders experience a 20% increase in employee job satisfaction.

This style of leadership focuses on inspiring and motivating employees to reach their full potential, creating a positive work environment where individuals feel valued and supported. Transformational leaders encourage creativity and innovation, fostering a culture of continuous improvement.

By providing clear goals and a sense of purpose, they empower their team members to take ownership of their work and strive for excellence. Additionally, transformational leaders prioritize communication, actively listening to their employees' concerns and ideas, and providing constructive feedback.

This open and transparent communication fosters trust and collaboration, resulting in higher levels of employee engagement and satisfaction. Overall, the implementation of transformational leadership not only enhances employee satisfaction but also improves organizational performance and success.

Chapter 3: Theories of Leadership

In Chapter 3, you'll explore three key theories of leadership: the Trait Theory, Behavioral Theories, and Contingency Theories.

The Trait Theory suggests that certain innate qualities or characteristics make someone a good leader.

Behavioral Theories focus on the actions and behaviors that leaders exhibit, emphasizing the importance of specific leadership styles.

Finally, Contingency Theories propose that effective leadership depends on the situation and the leader's ability to adapt their approach accordingly.

Understanding these theories will provide you with valuable insights and practical strategies for unleashing your true power as a leader.

Trait Theory of Leadership

In order to truly understand the power of leadership, it's important to delve into the Trait Theory.

This theory is based on the belief that certain inherent traits determine one's ability to lead effectively.

By understanding these traits, you can not only identify potential leaders, but also develop and enhance your own leadership skills.

Successful leaders possess a unique combination of traits such as confidence, adaptability, and integrity.

These traits enable them to inspire and influence others towards a common goal.

Basis of Theory

Contrary to popular belief, understanding the basis of theory is essential for unlocking the true power of leadership. When it comes to leadership, having a solid foundation of knowledge and understanding the underlying principles is crucial for effective decision-making and inspiring others.

The basis of theory provides leaders with a framework to analyze and interpret different situations, allowing them to make informed choices and adapt their leadership style accordingly. By delving into the basis of theory, leaders can gain insights into the various factors that influence leadership effectiveness, such as personality traits, behaviors, and situational dynamics.

This knowledge empowers leaders to identify their strengths and areas for improvement, enabling them to grow and develop as effective leaders. Furthermore, understanding the basis of theory helps leaders recognize the importance of continuous learning and development, as leadership is not a static concept but a lifelong journey of growth.

Therefore, by embracing the basis of theory, leaders can unlock their true potential and unleash the power of leadership to inspire and motivate others towards shared goals.

Understanding Traits

Understanding traits is key to unlocking the full potential of leadership. Research shows that individuals with high emotional intelligence are more likely to be successful leaders. A study revealed that leaders with high emotional intelligence outperform those with low emotional intelligence by 20%.

Emotional intelligence allows leaders to effectively navigate and manage their own emotions. It also helps them understand and empathize with the emotions of others. This skill enables leaders to build strong relationships, inspire and motivate their teams, and make informed decisions.

By recognizing and developing their emotional intelligence, leaders can enhance their ability to connect with others, foster a positive work environment, and drive greater overall success.

Traits of Successful Leaders

When it comes to being a successful leader, having a high level of emotional intelligence is crucial. Being able to understand and manage your own emotions, as well as empathize with and connect with others, is essential in building strong relationships and effectively leading a team.

Successful leaders are able to navigate through challenging situations with grace and composure, using their emotional intelligence to effectively communicate and resolve conflicts. They are able to inspire and motivate their team members, creating a positive and productive work environment.

Additionally, leaders with high emotional intelligence are able to adapt to change and make sound decisions based on their understanding of people's emotions and motivations. By cultivating emotional intelligence, leaders can unleash their true power and create a lasting impact on their teams and organizations.

Behavioral Theories of Leadership

In this discussion, you will explore the Behavioral Theories of Leadership, focusing on three key points:

- The basis of the theory is that effective leadership is not solely determined by inherent traits, but rather by the behaviors exhibited by leaders.

- Understanding behaviors and studying them can provide insights into what makes a successful leader and allow you to apply those practices in your own leadership journey.

- The leadership behavior framework provides a structured approach to analyzing and categorizing different leadership behaviors. It allows you to identify the most effective strategies for leading others.

Basis of Theory

To truly unleash the power of leadership, you must grasp the foundation of theory. The basis of leadership theory lies in understanding the behaviors and actions of leaders and how they impact their followers. By studying various behavioral theories of leadership, you can gain insights into the different styles and approaches that leaders can adopt.

This knowledge allows you to identify your own strengths and weaknesses as a leader, and leverage them to effectively motivate and inspire your team. Additionally, understanding the basis of theory helps you recognize the importance of adaptability and flexibility in leadership. Different situations call for different leadership styles, and by being aware of the theory behind leadership, you can adjust your approach to suit the needs of your team and organization.

Ultimately, having a strong foundation in leadership theory empowers you to become a more effective and influential leader, capable of driving positive change and achieving exceptional results.

Understanding Behaviors

Immerse yourself in the realm of leadership by delving into the intricate tapestry of behaviors and unlocking the key to understanding the dynamics that drive effective leaders.

By studying behaviors, you gain valuable insights into the actions, reactions, and interactions that shape a leader's effectiveness. Understanding behaviors allows you to decipher the underlying motivations, strengths, and weaknesses that influence a leader's decision-making process. It helps you identify patterns, spot potential obstacles, and develop strategies to overcome them.

By observing and analyzing behaviors, you can uncover hidden talents, cultivate leadership skills, and adapt your own approach to become a more effective leader.

It is through understanding behaviors that you can truly unleash the true power of leadership as you tap into the potential within yourself and others to create positive change and drive success.

Leadership Behavior Framework

Explore the intricacies of the Leadership Behavior Framework as it unveils the blueprint for understanding and mastering effective leadership behaviors.

This framework provides a comprehensive guide to the various behaviors that leaders exhibit and how they impact their teams and organizations. By understanding these behaviors, leaders can gain insights into their own strengths and areas for improvement. They can also learn how to adapt their behavior to different situations and individuals, maximizing their effectiveness as leaders.

The Leadership Behavior Framework offers practical tools and techniques for leaders to develop their skills and enhance their impact.

It emphasizes the importance of building trust, establishing clear communication, fostering collaboration, and inspiring others to achieve shared goals.

By utilizing this framework, leaders can unlock their true potential and unleash the power of their leadership beyond traditional authority.

Contingency Theories of Leadership

In exploring the Contingency Theories of Leadership, you'll delve into the basis of this theory. It focuses on the idea that effective leadership is contingent upon various factors.

One model within this theory is Fielder's Model. It emphasizes the importance of leadership style and situational favorability.

Hersey and Blanchard's Situational Theory expands on this. It emphasizes the need for leaders to adapt their style based on the readiness of their followers.

Lastly, the Path-Goal Theory suggests that effective leaders focus on clearing the path and providing guidance to help their followers achieve their goals.

Understanding these key points will help you develop a more nuanced understanding of leadership and its complexities.

Basis of Theory

Believe me, you won't find a more riveting basis of theory than the one I'm about to reveal to you.

The basis of contingency theories of leadership lies in the understanding that there is no one-size-fits-all approach to leadership. Instead, it emphasizes that effective leadership is contingent upon various factors such as the situation, the followers, and the leader's own attributes.

This theory acknowledges that different situations call for different leadership styles and that effective leaders are those who can adapt their approach based on the specific circumstances. It recognizes that what works in one situation may not work in another and that leaders need to be flexible and responsive.

By considering the unique dynamics of each situation, leaders can better understand how to motivate and inspire their followers, ultimately unleashing the true power of leadership.

Fielder's Model

Get ready to dive into the fascinating world of Fielder's Model, where you'll discover a fresh perspective on effective leadership that goes beyond traditional theories.

Developed by Fred E. Fielder in the 1960s, this model focuses on the interaction between a leader's style and the situational favorableness of the environment.

According to Fielder, a leader's style is either task-oriented or relationship-oriented, and this style is relatively fixed.

In contrast, the situational favorableness can be measured by three factors: leader-member relations, task structure, and position power.

Fielder's Model suggests that the effectiveness of a leader's style depends on the match between their style and the situational favorableness.

This means that a task-oriented leader would be most effective in highly favorable or highly unfavorable situations, while a relationship-oriented leader would excel in moderately favorable situations.

By understanding and applying Fielder's Model, leaders can gain valuable insights into their own style and adapt it to different situations, ultimately enhancing their effectiveness and achieving better results.

Hersey and Blanchard's Situational Theory

Discover the dynamic world of Hersey and Blanchard's Situational Theory, where you can learn how to adapt your leadership style based on the needs of your team and the specific situation at hand.

This theory recognizes that there's no one-size-fits-all approach to leadership, and instead emphasizes the importance of matching your leadership style to the development level of your team members.

By understanding the readiness and competence of your team, you can effectively choose between four leadership styles: telling, selling, participating, and delegating.

This theory encourages leaders to be flexible and responsive, enabling them to provide the right amount of support and direction to their team members.

By effectively applying this theory, you can foster a positive and productive work environment, where individuals feel empowered and motivated to excel.

So, embrace the power of situational leadership and unlock your true potential as a leader.

Path-Goal Theory

The Path-Goal Theory presents a practical approach to leadership, providing a clear path for you to guide and support your team members in achieving their goals.

According to this theory, as a leader, your primary responsibility is to remove any obstacles that may hinder your team's progress towards their objectives. You're expected to provide the necessary direction, support, and motivation to ensure that your team members understand the goals and have the means to achieve them.

This theory emphasizes the importance of adapting your leadership style to the needs and characteristics of your team members. By understanding their individual needs, preferences, and capabilities, you can tailor your approach to provide the right guidance and support.

Whether it's clarifying goals, offering incentives, or providing coaching, the Path-Goal Theory offers a practical framework to help you unleash the true potential of your team and achieve collective success.

Chapter 4: Emotional Intelligence and Leadership

In this chapter, you'll explore the importance of understanding emotional intelligence in the context of leadership. Discover how emotional intelligence can enhance your effectiveness as a leader and how it plays a crucial role in building strong relationships with your team members.

Gain practical insights on how to develop and cultivate your own emotional intelligence as a leader to create a positive and productive work environment.

Understanding Emotional Intelligence

In order to truly unleash the power of your leadership, it's essential to understand the key aspects of emotional intelligence.

Firstly, emotional recognition allows you to accurately identify and understand the emotions of yourself and those around you. This enables you to empathize and connect on a deeper level.

Secondly, emotion regulation is the ability to effectively manage and control your own emotions. It allows you to navigate challenging situations with composure and clarity.

Lastly, emotion utilization involves harnessing the power of emotions to motivate and inspire others. This creates a positive and productive work environment.

Emotional Recognition

Emotional recognition is key to unlocking the true power of leadership and connecting with others on a deeper level. By being able to recognize and understand the emotions of those around you, you can effectively communicate and empathize with them. This skill allows you to build strong relationships and create a positive and supportive work environment.

When you're able to recognize and acknowledge someone's emotions, it shows that you care and are truly present in the moment. It also helps you to navigate difficult situations and conflicts, as you can address the underlying emotions and work towards a resolution.

Emotional recognition isn't just about understanding others, but also about understanding yourself. By being aware of your own emotions and how they affect your actions, you can better manage your own behavior and make more informed decisions.

Ultimately, emotional recognition is a powerful tool that can help you become a more effective leader and create a positive impact in both your personal and professional life.

Emotion Regulation

Take control of your emotions and harness the power of emotion regulation to create a sense of calm and balance in your life.

Emotion regulation is the ability to effectively manage and control your emotions, allowing you to respond to situations in a more balanced and rational way.

When you can regulate your emotions, you are able to navigate through life's ups and downs with greater ease and resilience.

By recognizing and understanding your emotions, you can develop strategies to regulate them, such as deep breathing exercises, mindfulness techniques, or reframing negative thoughts.

Emotion regulation is a valuable skill that can help you to maintain healthy relationships, make better decisions, and improve your overall well-being.

So, take the time to tune into your emotions, learn how to regulate them, and unlock the true power of leadership within yourself.

Emotion Utilization

Utilizing our emotions effectively can be like harnessing the power of a raging river, guiding it towards a steady and purposeful flow. Emotion utilization is about understanding and leveraging the energy and information that our emotions provide, rather than suppressing or dismissing them.

By recognizing our emotions as valuable sources of insight, we can tap into their power to drive positive change and enhance our leadership abilities. Emotions can provide important signals about our values, needs, and desires, allowing us to make more informed decisions and connect with others on a deeper level.

When we embrace our emotions and use them as a tool for self-awareness and growth, we can become more authentic leaders who inspire and motivate those around us. Emotion utilization also involves effectively managing and expressing our emotions in a way that is constructive and productive, rather than destructive or harmful.

By channeling our emotions towards productive outcomes, we can create a positive and supportive work environment where everyone feels valued and empowered. Through emotion utilization, we can tap into the true power of leadership and unlock our full potential as leaders who make a meaningful impact.

Emotional Intelligence and Effective Leadership

When it comes to effective leadership, empathy plays a crucial role. Being able to understand and relate to the emotions of your team members allows you to build stronger relationships and create a supportive work environment.

Emotional stability is another key trait of successful leaders, as it enables them to remain calm under pressure and make rational decisions. By harnessing the power of empathy and emotional stability, you can unleash the true potential of your leadership and drive your team towards success.

Empathy in Leadership

Imagine being a leader who truly understands the needs and emotions of your team members, allowing you to create a supportive work environment where productivity flourishes. Studies show that teams led by empathetic leaders have a 50% higher level of employee engagement.

Empathy in leadership is a crucial skill that enables you to connect with your team on a deeper level, fostering trust and loyalty. By putting yourself in their shoes and genuinely listening to their concerns, you can address their needs effectively and provide the necessary support.

Empathetic leaders have the ability to recognize and validate their team members' emotions, which creates a safe space for open communication and collaboration. This understanding and compassion not only improves team dynamics but also boosts morale and motivation.

When employees feel understood and valued, they are more likely to go above and beyond, leading to increased productivity and overall success. So, as a leader, remember to practice empathy, and watch your team thrive in an environment where their voices are heard and their well-being is prioritized.

Emotional Stability and Leadership

Emotional stability is essential for effective leadership as it allows you to remain calm and composed in challenging situations, inspiring confidence and trust among your team members.

As a leader, your ability to regulate your emotions and maintain a level-headed approach is crucial in navigating through complex problems and making sound decisions.

When you display emotional stability, you create a sense of safety and security within your team, enabling them to perform at their best.

By controlling your own emotions, you can also be more attuned to the emotions of others, allowing you to empathize and connect with your team on a deeper level.

Moreover, emotional stability helps you handle conflicts and setbacks with resilience and grace, fostering a positive and productive work environment.

By demonstrating emotional stability, you set an example for your team, showing them how to manage their emotions and approach challenges with a clear and rational mindset.

Ultimately, your emotional stability as a leader not only impacts your own effectiveness but also influences the overall success and well-being of your team.

Building Emotional Intelligence as Leaders

To build emotional intelligence as leaders, you need to focus on skills development, training, and coaching.

By honing your skills, you can better understand and manage your emotions, as well as those of others.

Training and coaching can provide you with the tools and techniques to enhance your emotional intelligence, while practice scenarios allow you to apply these skills in real-life situations, further refining your abilities.

Skills Development

Developing skills isn't just about acquiring knowledge, but also about honing abilities and fostering growth.

As a leader, it's crucial to constantly work on developing your skills to stay ahead of the game. Whether it's improving your communication skills, expanding your technical knowledge, or enhancing your problem-solving abilities, skills development is essential for effective leadership.

By investing time and effort into skill-building, you can become a more confident and capable leader. One practical way to develop skills is through continuous learning and seeking opportunities for growth. This can involve attending workshops, taking online courses, or even seeking mentorship from experienced leaders.

Additionally, it's important to practice and apply your skills in real-life situations to reinforce your learning and improve your proficiency.

Remember, skills development is an ongoing process, and it requires dedication and perseverance. By investing in your own growth, you can unleash your true power as a leader and inspire others to do the same.

Training and Coaching

Now that you've honed your skills and developed a strong foundation, it's time to take your leadership to the next level through training and coaching.

This subtopic focuses on the invaluable role that training and coaching play in unleashing your true power as a leader. Training provides you with the necessary knowledge and tools to excel in your role, while coaching helps you refine your skills and overcome any obstacles that may arise.

By investing in both training and coaching, you'll gain the confidence and expertise needed to navigate complex leadership challenges with ease. Whether it's attending workshops, participating in leadership programs, or working with a personal coach, these resources will enable you to continually enhance your leadership abilities and reach new heights in your career.

Embrace the opportunity to learn and grow, and watch as your leadership potential flourishes.

Practice Scenarios

Experiencing practice scenarios is an effective way to solidify your leadership skills and navigate complex challenges with confidence. By immersing yourself in simulated situations, you can gain valuable hands-on experience and develop your decision-making abilities.

Practice scenarios allow you to test different strategies, explore various approaches, and learn from both successes and failures. This experiential learning helps you understand the nuances of leadership and prepares you to handle real-life situations more effectively.

Through practice scenarios, you can identify your strengths and weaknesses, refine your communication and problem-solving skills, and build resilience in the face of adversity. By actively engaging in these simulations, you can become more adaptable, enhance your leadership presence, and develop the confidence to lead with authority and authenticity.

So, embrace the opportunity to practice and immerse yourself in scenarios that mirror real-world challenges, as it's a practical and insightful way to unleash the true power of your leadership.

Chapter 5: Leadership Ethics

In Chapter 5, you'll explore the crucial topic of leadership ethics and its significance in effective leadership. Understanding the importance of ethics in leadership is vital because it provides a strong foundation for building trust, fostering positive relationships, and making ethical decisions. You'll also delve into the elements of ethical leadership, such as integrity, accountability, and fairness. These elements are essential in guiding ethical behavior and promoting a culture of ethical leadership within an organization.

Importance of Ethics in Leadership

When it comes to leadership, building trust is paramount. By demonstrating ethical behavior, you can establish a solid foundation of trust with your team, fostering loyalty and collaboration.

Additionally, ethics play a crucial role in enhancing your reputation as a leader, as people are more likely to follow and respect those who consistently make ethical decisions.

Lastly, ethics also have legal implications, as leaders who act unethically can face severe consequences such as lawsuits or damage to their organization's reputation.

Therefore, it's crucial to prioritize ethics in leadership to unleash the true power of your influence.

Building Trust

Trust is crucial for effective leadership, as it empowers individuals to fully engage and collaborate towards a common goal. When people trust their leaders, they're more likely to share their ideas, take risks, and work together as a team.

Building trust requires leaders to be transparent, honest, and consistent in their actions and communication. It's essential to keep promises and follow through on commitments. Leaders should also be open to feedback and actively listen to their team members.

By creating a culture of trust, leaders can foster an environment where everyone feels valued and respected, and where innovation and creativity can thrive. Trust is the foundation of successful leadership, and by prioritizing it, leaders can unleash the true power of their teams.

Enhancing Reputation

To enhance your reputation, you must carefully craft a persona that's both authentic and captivating, allowing others to see the true value and potential you possess. Your reputation isn't just about what others think of you, but also about how you present yourself to the world.

It's important to be consistent in your actions and words, as this will build trust and credibility. Take the time to understand your strengths and weaknesses, and focus on showcasing your strengths in a way that's genuine and appealing. Remember to be transparent and honest in your interactions, as this will help establish a solid foundation for your reputation.

Additionally, it's crucial to deliver on your promises and exceed expectations whenever possible. This will not only enhance your reputation but also create a sense of reliability and dependability.

Lastly, actively seek feedback and listen to the opinions of others. This will allow you to continuously improve and adapt, ultimately contributing to a stronger and more positive reputation.

Legal Implications

Explore the legal implications and consequences that can arise from actions and decisions you make, ensuring you understand the potential ramifications of your choices.

As a leader, it's crucial to be aware of the legal landscape in which you operate. Any misstep or oversight could have serious legal ramifications, potentially leading to lawsuits, fines, or even criminal charges.

By taking the time to understand the laws and regulations that apply to your industry, you can make informed decisions that minimize legal risks.

It's also important to consult with legal experts when necessary, as they can provide valuable guidance and help you navigate complex legal issues.

Remember, the legal implications of your actions extend not only to yourself but also to your team and organization as a whole. Therefore, it's essential to prioritize compliance and ensure that your actions align with legal requirements.

By being proactive and mindful of the legal implications of your decisions, you can protect yourself, your team, and your organization from unnecessary legal trouble.

Elements of Ethical Leadership

When it comes to ethical leadership, three key elements stand out: integrity, accountability, and fairness.

These are the building blocks that not only define a leader's character but also determine the success of their leadership.

By embodying integrity, you demonstrate honesty and strong moral principles, earning the trust and respect of your team.

Accountability ensures that you take responsibility for your actions and decisions, fostering a culture of transparency and growth.

Lastly, fairness ensures that everyone is treated equitably, fostering a positive and inclusive work environment.

Integrity

Integrity is the cornerstone of effective leadership, allowing you to inspire trust and create lasting impact. When you lead with integrity, you consistently align your actions with your values and principles.

This consistency builds trust among your team members, as they see that you are true to your word and that you always act in the best interests of the organization.

Integrity also fosters a culture of transparency and accountability, as you hold yourself and others to high ethical standards. By demonstrating integrity in your leadership, you set an example for others to follow, encouraging them to act with honesty and integrity as well.

Ultimately, integrity is not just about doing the right thing when others are watching, but also when no one is. It's about staying true to your values even in the face of challenges and difficult decisions.

So, embrace integrity as a fundamental aspect of your leadership style, and watch as it empowers you to make a positive and lasting impact on your team and organization.

Accountability

Accountability is essential in effective leadership, as it fosters a culture of transparency and trust among team members. According to a study by Gallup, organizations with high levels of accountability are 2.5 times more likely to have engaged employees.

When leaders hold themselves and their team members accountable, it sets a standard of excellence and creates a sense of ownership and responsibility. This leads to increased productivity, better problem-solving, and a stronger commitment to achieving goals.

Accountability also allows leaders to identify areas for improvement and provide constructive feedback, which helps individuals grow and develop professionally. By emphasizing accountability, leaders create a supportive environment where everyone feels valued and motivated to contribute their best.

They encourage open communication, collaboration, and a shared commitment to success. Ultimately, accountability is not about pointing fingers or assigning blame; it's about taking ownership and working together to achieve collective goals.

So, as a leader, embrace accountability and inspire your team to do the same, as it's the key to unleashing the true power of leadership.

Fairness

Fairness in leadership creates a level playing field and fosters an inclusive and harmonious work environment where everyone feels valued and respected. When leaders prioritize fairness, they ensure that decisions and actions are based on objective criteria, without any bias or favoritism.

This not only promotes transparency but also encourages trust among team members. Fairness in leadership means treating everyone equally, regardless of their background, position, or personal relationships. It means providing opportunities for growth and development to all individuals, based on their skills and merit.

By embracing fairness, leaders can create a culture of accountability and encourage open communication, where employees feel comfortable speaking up and expressing their opinions. This ultimately leads to better collaboration, enhanced productivity, and a more engaged workforce.

Chapter 6: Developing Leadership Skills

In this chapter, you'll explore the importance of identifying key leadership skills and how to develop them.

You'll learn practical strategies for building and enhancing your leadership skills, allowing you to become a more effective and influential leader.

Additionally, you'll discover the significance of assessing your leadership skills to gauge your progress and identify areas for improvement.

Identifying Key Leadership Skills

In order to unleash the true power of leadership, it's crucial to identify and develop key skills. These skills include communication, decision making, and delegation. Effective communication is essential for building relationships, fostering trust, and conveying a clear vision to your team. Making informed and timely decisions is vital for navigating challenges and achieving goals. Additionally, delegating tasks and responsibilities empowers your team, promotes growth, and allows you to focus on strategic priorities.

Communication

Effective communication is not just about conveying information, but rather about fostering genuine connection and understanding among individuals. It is the key to building strong relationships, both personally and professionally.

When you communicate effectively, you are able to express your thoughts and ideas clearly, listen actively to others, and find common ground. It involves not just speaking, but also actively listening and empathizing with others.

By using active voice and contractions, you can make your communication more engaging and relatable.

Remember that effective communication is a skill that can be learned and improved upon with practice. So, take the time to develop your communication skills and unleash the true power of leadership.

Decision Making

When you make decisions, you have the power to shape your own future and create the life you truly desire. Decision making is a crucial aspect of leadership, as it requires careful analysis, critical thinking, and the ability to weigh different options.

Effective decision making involves gathering relevant information, evaluating potential outcomes, and considering the long-term implications. It's important to trust your instincts and listen to your gut, but also to seek input from others and consider different perspectives.

By making well-informed decisions, you can navigate through challenges, seize opportunities, and lead with confidence. Remember, every decision you make has the potential to impact not only yourself but also those around you.

So, take the time to think through your choices and make decisions that align with your values and goals.

Delegation

Entrusting others with responsibilities and tasks, delegation allows you to distribute the workload and foster a sense of teamwork and collaboration.

By delegating tasks to your team members, you're not only lightening your own load but also empowering them to take ownership and contribute to the success of the project or organization.

Delegation is an essential skill for effective leadership as it allows you to focus on strategic decision-making and higher-level responsibilities, while also providing opportunities for your team members to grow and develop their skills.

However, it's important to delegate effectively by clearly communicating expectations, providing necessary resources and support, and regularly checking in to ensure progress is being made.

Delegation not only benefits the leader but also the team as it builds trust, improves efficiency, and encourages innovation.

So, embrace the power of delegation and watch your team thrive.

Building Leadership Skills

If you're looking to enhance your leadership skills, there are various programs available that can help you achieve your goals. Skill enhancement programs offer a structured approach to developing and refining your leadership abilities, providing you with valuable tools and strategies.

Additionally, having role models and mentors can greatly contribute to your growth as a leader. They can provide guidance, support, and inspiration.

Lastly, self-study and continuous learning are essential for honing your leadership skills. They allow you to stay updated with the latest trends and best practices in the field.

Skill Enhancement Programs

Skill enhancement programs can significantly improve your leadership abilities. Studies show that participants experienced a 25% increase in their decision-making skills after completing such programs.

These programs provide a practical and insightful approach to developing your leadership skills. They offer a range of tools and techniques that can be applied in real-life situations.

By participating in these programs, you can learn how to effectively communicate your vision, motivate your team, and make better decisions.

Through interactive workshops, case studies, and role-playing exercises, you can gain a deeper understanding of different leadership styles and strategies.

Moreover, these programs often provide opportunities for networking and collaboration with other aspiring leaders. This allows you to learn from their experiences and broaden your perspectives.

Investing in skill enhancement programs is a proactive step towards unleashing your true leadership potential and taking your career to new heights.

Role models and Mentoring

Look for someone who embodies the qualities you aspire to have as a leader and can guide you through their experiences and knowledge.

Having a role model or mentor can be immensely beneficial in your journey towards becoming a successful leader.

They can provide valuable insights, offer guidance, and share their wisdom gained from years of experience. By observing and learning from their actions, you can gain a deeper understanding of effective leadership techniques and strategies.

A role model or mentor can also provide you with a sense of direction, helping you navigate through challenges and make informed decisions. They can inspire and motivate you to push beyond your limits and achieve your full potential as a leader.

So, take the time to find someone who can serve as your role model or mentor, and make the most of their guidance and support on your path to leadership excellence.

Self-study and Continuous Learning

Immerse yourself in self-study and embrace the mindset of continuous learning to constantly expand your knowledge and develop the essential qualities of a successful leader.

By engaging in self-study, you have the opportunity to delve deep into various topics, exploring and gaining insights that can enhance your leadership skills.

Take advantage of resources such as books, articles, online courses, and podcasts to broaden your understanding and stay updated with the latest trends and developments in your field.

Furthermore, make it a habit to reflect on your own experiences and learn from both successes and failures.

Continuous learning requires a growth mindset, a willingness to step outside of your comfort zone, and an eagerness to seek feedback and input from others.

As you engage in self-study and embrace continuous learning, you will not only enhance your own knowledge and skills but also inspire and motivate those around you to follow suit.

Assessing Leadership Skills

When it comes to assessing your leadership skills, there are three key points to consider:

- Feedback mechanisms allow you to receive valuable input from others and make necessary adjustments to your leadership style.

- Setting clear goals helps you stay focused and gives you something to strive for.

- Monitoring progress ensures that you are on track and making the necessary improvements.

By incorporating these key points into your leadership assessment, you can continuously improve and unleash the true power of your leadership.

Feedback Mechanisms

To truly unleash the true power of your leadership, you must embrace feedback mechanisms and understand that constructive criticism is essential for personal growth and improvement.

Feedback mechanisms provide valuable insights into your leadership style and behavior, allowing you to identify areas of strength and areas that need improvement.

By actively seeking feedback from your team, colleagues, and even superiors, you can gain a deeper understanding of how your actions and decisions impact those around you. This feedback can help you identify blind spots, challenge your assumptions, and ultimately become a more effective leader.

It's important to approach feedback with an open mind, viewing it as an opportunity for growth rather than a personal attack. Actively listen to the feedback provided, ask clarifying questions, and seek specific examples to better understand the areas that require improvement.

Once you have received feedback, take the time to reflect on it and develop an action plan to address the identified areas.

By incorporating feedback into your leadership approach, you won't only enhance your own development but also create a culture of continuous improvement within your team.

Remember, leadership isn't about having all the answers; it's about constantly learning and evolving to become a better leader for the benefit of your team and organization.

Goal Setting

Set ambitious goals that stretch your capabilities and push you to reach new heights, allowing you to soar above the clouds and achieve extraordinary success as a leader.

Goal setting is a crucial aspect of effective leadership, as it provides direction and focus for both individual and team efforts. By setting clear and challenging goals, you create a sense of purpose and motivation, inspiring yourself and others to work towards a common objective.

It's important to ensure that your goals are specific, measurable, achievable, relevant, and time-bound (SMART), as this will help you track progress and make necessary adjustments along the way.

Additionally, it's essential to communicate your goals to your team and involve them in the goal-setting process, fostering collaboration and commitment.

Remember, setting ambitious goals not only drives personal growth and development but also enables you to lead by example and inspire others to unleash their true potential.

So, dream big, set audacious goals, and watch as you and your team achieve extraordinary success.

Monitoring Progress

Keep your eyes on the prize and stay vigilant in monitoring progress towards your goals, like a hawk soaring high above its prey.

Monitoring progress is a crucial aspect of effective goal setting, as it allows you to track your performance, identify any deviations, and make necessary adjustments along the way.

By regularly assessing your progress, you can ensure that you stay on track and maintain the necessary momentum towards achieving your desired outcomes.

Monitoring progress also provides you with valuable insights into your strengths and weaknesses, allowing you to capitalize on your strengths and address any areas that may require improvement.

It helps you stay accountable to yourself and keeps you motivated by providing tangible evidence of your progress.

Additionally, monitoring progress enables you to celebrate milestones and small wins, which can further boost your confidence and drive.

So, make it a habit to regularly assess and monitor your progress towards your goals, and use the information you gather to make informed decisions and stay focused on your journey towards success.

Chapter 7: Leadership and Diversity

In this chapter, you'll explore the importance of understanding diversity in leadership. You'll learn how diversity can have a significant impact on leadership effectiveness and how it can bring a range of perspectives and experiences to the table.

Additionally, you'll discover strategies for promoting diversity in leadership roles, ensuring that a variety of voices are represented and heard.

Understanding Diversity in Leadership

In today's discussion, we'll delve into the importance of understanding diversity in leadership, going beyond mere authority and unlocking the true power of leadership.

We'll explore three key points: cultural diversity, gender diversity, and diversity of thought. By embracing these aspects, you'll gain valuable insights, enhance innovation, and foster an inclusive and dynamic leadership environment.

Cultural Diversity

Embrace the richness of cultural diversity and unlock the true potential of your leadership abilities.

In today's globalized world, cultural diversity is not just a buzzword, but a reality that leaders must navigate. By understanding and appreciating the various cultural backgrounds of your team members, you can create an inclusive and harmonious work environment that fosters innovation and collaboration.

Recognize that cultural diversity brings different perspectives, ideas, and approaches to problem-solving, which can lead to more well-rounded and effective decision-making. Take the time to learn about different cultures, their customs, traditions, and values, and incorporate this knowledge into your leadership style.

By doing so, you will not only gain the respect and trust of your diverse team, but also tap into their unique strengths and talents. Encourage open communication and create opportunities for cultural exchange, allowing team members to share their experiences and learn from one another.

By embracing cultural diversity, you will not only enhance your own leadership skills but also create a workplace that celebrates and thrives on the power of differences.

Gender Diversity

Now that we've explored the importance of cultural diversity in leadership, let's delve into another critical aspect: gender diversity.

Gender diversity refers to the inclusion of individuals of different genders in leadership positions. It recognizes the unique perspectives, experiences, and approaches that individuals of different genders can bring to the table.

Embracing gender diversity isn't just about achieving equality; it's about unlocking the full potential of leadership by tapping into the diverse talents and perspectives that exist in our society.

By actively promoting gender diversity, organizations can foster innovation, enhance decision-making processes, and create a more inclusive and dynamic work environment.

It's crucial for leaders to recognize the value of gender diversity and take proactive steps to ensure equal opportunities for all genders.

Diversity of Thought

Imagine the innovative ideas and creative solutions that can emerge when diverse perspectives come together in leadership positions. Don't you want to tap into the power of diversity of thought?

When you have a team that brings together individuals with different backgrounds, experiences, and ways of thinking, you open up a world of possibilities. Diversity of thought allows for a broader range of perspectives, which leads to a more comprehensive understanding of complex problems and the ability to come up with unique solutions.

By embracing diversity of thought, you create an environment where individuals feel comfortable challenging the status quo, thinking outside the box, and bringing new insights to the table. This not only fosters innovation but also enhances decision-making processes, as it reduces the risk of groupthink and encourages critical thinking.

In a rapidly changing world, where adaptability and agility are key to success, harnessing the power of diversity of thought is essential for effective leadership. It enables leaders to navigate uncertainty, identify opportunities, and drive growth by leveraging the full potential of their team.

So, why limit yourself to a narrow range of perspectives when you can tap into the wealth of ideas and perspectives that diversity of thought brings? Embrace the power of diversity and unlock the true potential of your leadership.

Impact of Diversity on Leadership

When it comes to team dynamics, diversity in leadership plays a crucial role. With a diverse group of leaders, different perspectives and ideas are brought to the table, leading to more effective problem-solving and decision-making.

Additionally, diversity in leadership fosters a sense of competitiveness within the team, as individuals strive to excel and contribute their unique skills and experiences.

Lastly, the impact of diversity on leadership is evident in the realm of innovation, where diverse leaders bring fresh insights and creative thinking to drive organizational growth and adaptability.

Team Dynamics

Team dynamics can make or break a project's success, so it's crucial for leaders to foster collaboration and open communication.

When a team is able to work together effectively, it can lead to increased productivity, creativity, and problem-solving.

However, if team dynamics are not managed properly, it can result in conflicts, lack of motivation, and a breakdown in communication.

To ensure positive team dynamics, leaders should encourage open dialogue and create an environment where everyone feels comfortable expressing their ideas and concerns.

It's essential for leaders to actively listen to their team members, provide constructive feedback, and resolve any conflicts that may arise.

Additionally, leaders should promote diversity within the team, as different perspectives can lead to better decision-making and innovation.

By prioritizing team dynamics, leaders can unleash the true power of their team and achieve remarkable results.

Competitiveness

Competitiveness is a key factor in driving innovation and success in organizations. Studies show that companies that prioritize competitiveness are 2.5 times more likely to be high performers.

Being competitive means constantly pushing yourself and your team to do better, to strive for excellence. It encourages a culture of continuous improvement and motivates individuals to go beyond their limits.

When you foster a competitive environment, you create a healthy sense of urgency and drive, pushing your team members to deliver their best work. It also encourages collaboration and teamwork as individuals strive to outperform each other in a constructive and supportive manner.

By embracing competitiveness, you can unleash the true potential of your team and achieve remarkable results. So, don't shy away from embracing a competitive mindset, as it can be a powerful tool for driving success in your organization.

Innovation

Embrace the spirit of innovation and watch as new ideas and creative solutions propel you and your organization to greater success.

In today's fast-paced and ever-changing business landscape, innovation isn't just a buzzword, but a necessity for survival.

By fostering a culture of innovation, you open the door to endless possibilities and opportunities for growth.

Encourage your team to think outside the box, to experiment, and to take calculated risks.

Embrace failure as a stepping stone to success, knowing that each setback brings valuable lessons and insights.

Foster an environment where diverse perspectives are welcomed, as this diversity fuels innovation.

Stay curious and constantly seek out new knowledge and experiences.

Embrace technology and leverage it to your advantage.

Embracing innovation means constantly challenging the status quo and pushing boundaries.

It means being open to change and adapting quickly.

It means being agile and responsive to the ever-evolving needs and expectations of your customers.

By embracing the spirit of innovation, you unleash the true power of leadership and position yourself and your organization as pioneers in your industry.

Promoting Diversity in Leadership Roles

When it comes to promoting diversity in leadership roles, there are three key points to consider: inclusive recruitment, leadership development programs, and equal opportunity initiatives.

Inclusive recruitment involves actively seeking out and hiring individuals from diverse backgrounds, ensuring that a range of perspectives are represented at the leadership level.

Leadership development programs provide training and support to individuals from underrepresented groups, helping them to develop the skills and confidence needed to take on leadership roles.

Equal opportunity initiatives aim to create a level playing field for all individuals, regardless of their background, by implementing policies and practices that promote fairness and inclusivity.

By focusing on these key points, organizations can create a more diverse and inclusive leadership landscape.

Inclusive Recruitment

Diversity in your recruitment efforts can lead to a stronger and more innovative team, but have you considered the full potential of inclusive recruitment? Inclusive recruitment goes beyond simply hiring a diverse workforce; it involves creating a culture and processes that actively seek out and welcome individuals from all backgrounds.

By embracing inclusive recruitment practices, you open up opportunities for a wider range of talent and perspectives, which can lead to increased creativity, problem-solving, and overall team performance. Inclusive recruitment also helps to break down barriers and biases that may exist within your organization, fostering a more inclusive and equitable workplace.

To implement inclusive recruitment, consider reviewing your job descriptions and requirements to ensure they are inclusive and do not unintentionally exclude certain groups. Additionally, diversify your recruitment sources and networks to reach a wider pool of candidates. Finally, create a supportive and inclusive interview process that allows candidates to showcase their skills and potential, regardless of their background.

By embracing inclusive recruitment, you can tap into the full potential of talent and create a more diverse and innovative team.

Leadership Development Programs

Leadership development programs are an effective way to cultivate and nurture a diverse pool of talented individuals, fostering a culture of growth and excellence.

These programs provide individuals with the opportunity to enhance their leadership skills, broaden their perspectives, and gain valuable insights into different industries and organizational dynamics.

Through experiential learning, mentorship, and targeted training, participants can develop the necessary competencies to lead effectively in today's complex and rapidly-changing business landscape.

Leadership development programs also offer a platform for networking and collaboration, enabling individuals to connect with like-minded peers and industry experts.

By investing in these programs, organizations not only enhance their leadership pipeline but also create a culture of continuous learning and innovation.

These programs empower individuals to unlock their full potential and maximize their impact, ultimately driving organizational success.

Equal Opportunity Initiatives

Equal opportunity initiatives level the playing field and create a fair and inclusive environment for all individuals to thrive and succeed. These initiatives aim to remove any barriers or biases that may exist in the workplace, ensuring that everyone has an equal chance to advance and contribute their unique talents and perspectives.

By promoting diversity and inclusion, organizations can tap into a wider pool of talent, fostering innovation and creativity. Equal opportunity initiatives also help to address systemic inequalities and promote social justice, allowing individuals from all backgrounds to have access to the same opportunities and resources.

Implementing these initiatives requires a commitment from leadership to challenge their own biases, create policies that promote fairness, and provide training and support to ensure everyone is aware of the importance of equal opportunity. Ultimately, by embracing equal opportunity initiatives, organizations can create a more harmonious and productive work environment, where everyone feels valued and empowered to reach their full potential.

Chapter 8: Conflict Resolution and Leadership

In Chapter 8, you'll explore the nature of conflicts in leadership roles and techniques for conflict resolution. You'll also discover the crucial role that leadership plays in resolving conflicts. Understanding the nature of conflicts in leadership roles is essential for effective resolution. It allows you to identify the underlying issues and address them accordingly. Techniques for conflict resolution will equip you with practical strategies to navigate and resolve conflicts. This fosters a harmonious and productive work environment. Ultimately, as a leader, your ability to actively engage in conflict resolution is vital in maintaining a positive and cohesive team dynamic.

Nature of Conflicts in Leadership Roles

In leadership roles, conflicts often arise in the form of individual disputes, team disagreements, and organizational conflicts. You'll find yourself dealing with individuals who may challenge your authority or question your decisions, requiring effective communication and conflict resolution skills.

Team disagreements can stem from varying opinions and approaches, and as a leader, it's important to foster a collaborative environment where all perspectives are respected.

Additionally, organizational conflicts can arise due to conflicting goals, limited resources, or power struggles, requiring you to navigate complex dynamics and find solutions that benefit the entire organization.

Individual Disputes

Unleash the true power of your leadership by addressing individual disputes, for they're the hidden thorns that hinder progress and unity, like weeds choking a flourishing garden.

As a leader, it's essential to recognize that individual disputes can arise within your team, and it's your responsibility to handle them effectively.

These disputes can stem from a variety of reasons, such as conflicting personalities, differences in opinions, or misunderstandings.

Ignoring or avoiding these disputes will only allow them to fester and grow, ultimately causing a negative impact on team dynamics and productivity.

To address individual disputes, start by creating an open and safe environment where team members feel comfortable expressing their concerns.

Actively listen to both sides of the dispute and encourage open dialogue to ensure that all perspectives are heard.

Seek to understand the underlying causes of the dispute and work towards finding a resolution that's fair and equitable.

Provide guidance and support to help individuals develop effective communication and conflict resolution skills.

By proactively addressing individual disputes, you can foster a culture of trust, collaboration, and growth within your team, unlocking the true potential of your leadership and paving the way for progress and unity.

Team Disagreements

Address team disagreements head-on by fostering open communication and encouraging collaboration, as they can hinder progress and unity within your team.

When team members have conflicting opinions or ideas, it is important to create a safe space where everyone feels comfortable expressing their thoughts and concerns.

Encourage active listening and respectful dialogue, allowing everyone to share their perspectives without fear of judgment or retribution.

By promoting open communication, you can uncover the root causes of the disagreements and work towards finding a common ground or solution.

Additionally, fostering collaboration can help team members recognize the value of different viewpoints and leverage each other's strengths to achieve shared goals.

Encourage team members to work together on projects, delegate tasks, and seek input from one another.

By embracing teamwork and collaboration, you can harness the collective intelligence of the team and overcome disagreements, leading to increased productivity and a stronger sense of unity.

Organizational Conflicts

Tackle organizational conflicts head-on by actively engaging in conflict resolution strategies, such as mediation or negotiation, to ensure a harmonious work environment.

For example, imagine you're a team leader faced with a conflict between two team members who have differing opinions on the best approach for a project. By facilitating a discussion where both individuals can express their perspectives and find common ground, you can help resolve the conflict and foster a sense of unity within the team.

It's important to create an environment where open communication is encouraged, allowing team members to voice their concerns and work towards mutually beneficial solutions.

Additionally, providing training and resources on conflict resolution techniques can equip individuals with the necessary skills to effectively address and manage conflicts.

By addressing organizational conflicts proactively, you can minimize their negative impact and promote a positive and productive work culture.

Techniques for Conflict Resolution

When it comes to resolving conflicts in leadership roles, there are three key techniques that you should consider: mediation, negotiation, and decision making.

Mediation involves bringing in a neutral third party to help facilitate a conversation and find a resolution that satisfies everyone involved.

Negotiation allows for a give-and-take approach, where each party can express their needs and work towards a compromise.

Finally, decision making involves making a firm choice or taking action to resolve a conflict, even if it means not everyone will be completely satisfied.

By utilizing these techniques, you can effectively address conflicts in your leadership role and foster a more harmonious and productive environment.

Mediation

Engaging in mediation allows you to tap into your true power as a leader and resolve conflicts in a collaborative and constructive manner. Mediation is a powerful technique that enables you to bring conflicting parties together and facilitate a productive conversation.

By actively listening to both sides and guiding the discussion, you create a safe space for open communication and understanding. Through mediation, you can uncover the underlying issues and interests of each party, helping them find common ground and reach a mutually beneficial solution.

This approach not only resolves conflicts but also strengthens relationships and fosters a positive work environment. Mediation empowers you as a leader to address conflicts head-on, promote teamwork, and create a culture of trust and respect.

Negotiation

Negotiation allows leaders to leverage their communication skills and find mutually beneficial solutions, but how can you ensure that all parties involved are satisfied with the outcome?

The key lies in understanding the interests and needs of each party and finding common ground. Effective negotiation involves active listening, empathy, and creative problem-solving. By actively engaging with each party and understanding their motivations, you can work towards a solution that meets everyone's needs.

It's important to approach negotiations with an open mind and a willingness to compromise. By focusing on the bigger picture and the long-term benefits, leaders can create win-win situations that foster collaboration and build stronger relationships.

Remember, negotiation is not about winning or losing, but about finding a solution that satisfies everyone involved.

Decision Making

To make effective decisions, you must trust your instincts and listen to your heart, as it's often in those moments of vulnerability that the most authentic and impactful choices are made.

Decision making is not just about analyzing data and weighing pros and cons; it requires tapping into your intuition and understanding your own values and beliefs.

Sometimes, the logical choice may seem clear, but deep down, you may feel a sense of unease or conflict. In these instances, it's essential to listen to your inner voice, as it may be guiding you towards a decision that aligns with your true self.

Additionally, being aware of your emotions and how they influence your decision-making process is crucial. Emotions can provide valuable insights and help you consider different perspectives. However, it's important to strike a balance between emotions and rationality, ensuring that your decisions are well-informed and grounded in reality.

Ultimately, effective decision making requires a combination of intuition, emotional intelligence, and practical reasoning. By trusting your instincts and listening to your heart, you can make decisions that are not only impactful but also authentic to who you are as a leader.

Role of Leadership in Conflict Resolution

When it comes to conflict resolution, as a leader, your role is crucial. You have the power to set a positive tone for the entire team, which can greatly impact how conflicts are approached and resolved.

Additionally, you must facilitate effective communication between the parties involved, ensuring that everyone's perspectives are heard and understood.

Lastly, as a leader, it's your responsibility to implement fair solutions that address the root causes of the conflict and promote harmony within the team.

Setting a Positive Tone

Creating a positive tone from the start allows you, as a leader, to unleash your true power and captivate your audience.

When you set a positive tone, you create an environment that fosters collaboration, trust, and open communication.

By being approachable and encouraging, you create a space where team members feel comfortable sharing their ideas and concerns.

This positive tone sets the stage for effective conflict resolution, as it promotes understanding and empathy among team members.

It also helps to build strong relationships, which are essential for successful leadership.

When you start on a positive note, you inspire others to follow your lead and create a culture of positivity and productivity.

So, take the time to set a positive tone from the beginning and watch as your leadership potential flourishes.

Facilitating Communication

By fostering open communication, you become the bridge that connects individuals and facilitates the flow of ideas within your team.

As a leader, it's crucial to create an environment where team members feel comfortable expressing their thoughts, opinions, and concerns.

Encourage open dialogue by actively listening to your team members, asking for their input, and valuing their contributions.

By doing so, you not only promote collaboration and innovation but also build trust and strengthen relationships among team members.

Effective communication also involves providing clear expectations, giving constructive feedback, and addressing conflicts promptly and respectfully.

By facilitating communication, you empower your team to share ideas, solve problems, and work together towards achieving common goals.

Implementing Fair Solutions

Implementing fair solutions is essential for fostering a harmonious and equitable work environment. When leaders prioritize fairness, they demonstrate a commitment to treating all employees with respect and dignity.

Fair solutions involve considering the needs and perspectives of all parties involved and making decisions that are unbiased and impartial. By implementing fair solutions, leaders not only promote a sense of fairness but also encourage trust and loyalty among their team members.

When employees feel that their concerns and grievances are being addressed in a fair and just manner, they are more likely to be engaged and motivated in their work. Fair solutions also help to prevent conflicts and promote effective communication within the organization.

By considering different viewpoints and ensuring that decisions are based on objective criteria, leaders can create a culture of fairness and accountability, where everyone feels valued and heard. Implementing fair solutions is not just about following rules and regulations, but about creating a work environment where every individual feels empowered and respected.

Chapter 9: Leadership in Different Contexts

In Chapter 9, you'll explore the concept of leadership in different contexts. This includes corporate, political, and community leadership. Understanding the unique challenges and dynamics of each context is essential for effective leadership. You'll gain insights on how to navigate these different environments, inspire others, and make a positive impact in diverse settings.

Corporate Leadership

In corporate leadership, it's crucial to understand the impact of business strategy, workforce management, and financial decisions.

These key points are interconnected and play a significant role in unleashing the true power of leadership beyond authority.

By aligning business strategy with the goals and objectives of the organization, leaders can effectively guide their teams towards success.

Additionally, effective workforce management ensures that the right people are in the right roles, fostering productivity and growth.

Finally, making informed financial decisions enables leaders to allocate resources wisely, driving profitability and long-term sustainability.

Business Strategy

Crafting a successful business strategy involves tapping into the untapped potential of your organization.

In order to do this, it's essential to have a clear understanding of your company's strengths, weaknesses, opportunities, and threats.

By conducting a thorough analysis of your internal and external environment, you can identify areas where your organization can excel and areas where it may need improvement.

Additionally, it's important to align your business strategy with your overall goals and objectives. This involves setting realistic targets, developing a clear plan of action, and regularly reviewing and adjusting your strategy as necessary.

By taking these steps, you can unleash the true power of leadership and drive your organization towards success.

Workforce Management

Managing your workforce is like conducting an orchestra, where each individual brings a unique talent that, when coordinated effectively, creates a harmonious and powerful performance. As a leader, it's crucial to understand the strengths and weaknesses of your team members and allocate tasks accordingly.

By doing so, you can ensure that each person is working on something they excel at, maximizing productivity and job satisfaction. Additionally, effective workforce management involves clear communication and regular feedback. Regular check-ins and performance evaluations enable you to recognize and reward your team's achievements while also providing constructive criticism to help them grow.

Emphasizing a positive and collaborative work environment fosters motivation and loyalty among your employees, leading to higher retention rates and overall success. Moreover, it's essential to provide opportunities for professional development and training to enhance the skills and knowledge of your workforce. By investing in their growth, you not only develop a more capable team but also demonstrate your commitment to their success.

In conclusion, effective workforce management is a critical aspect of leadership that, when done right, can unlock the true potential of your team and drive your organization towards success.

Financial Decisions

Now that you've learned about effective workforce management, it's time to delve into the realm of financial decisions. As a leader, you have the power to influence and shape the financial direction of your organization.

From budgeting and resource allocation to investment decisions and financial planning, your choices have a direct impact on the success and growth of your company.

By understanding the financial landscape and making informed decisions, you can optimize your organization's financial performance and ensure its long-term sustainability. It's crucial to analyze financial data, monitor key performance indicators, and collaborate with financial experts to make sound financial decisions.

By doing so, you can unleash the true power of your leadership and steer your organization towards greater success.

Political Leadership

When it comes to political leadership, there are three key points that you need to keep in mind: public policy, public communication, and crisis management.

Public policy is all about making decisions that directly affect the lives of the people you serve, so it's crucial to understand their needs and concerns.

Effective public communication is essential for building trust and gaining support from the public, while crisis management is about being able to navigate through difficult situations and make quick, informed decisions.

By mastering these key points, you'll be well-equipped to lead effectively in the political arena.

Public Policy

Unlock the true power of your leadership by embracing the potential for change and innovation in public policy. As a leader, it's crucial to recognize the impact that public policy can have on your organization and the community at large.

By actively engaging in the public policy process, you can shape the decisions and regulations that directly affect your industry. This involvement allows you to not only advocate for your organization's interests but also contribute to the overall betterment of society.

Public policy provides a platform for you to address important issues, promote social justice, and drive positive change. It's through this process that you can demonstrate your leadership skills and make a lasting impact on the world around you.

So, don't shy away from getting involved in public policy discussions and initiatives. Take the initiative to understand the issues, build relationships with key stakeholders, and articulate your organization's perspective. By doing so, you can unleash the true power of your leadership and create a brighter future for all.

Public Communication

Embrace the power of effective public communication as a key to open doors of understanding and bridge gaps between diverse perspectives.

In today's fast-paced and interconnected world, public communication plays a crucial role in shaping opinions, influencing decisions, and fostering collaboration.

It's not enough to simply convey information; leaders must master the art of engaging with their audience, capturing their attention, and delivering their message with clarity and impact.

By understanding the needs, values, and concerns of different stakeholders, leaders can tailor their communication strategies to resonate with their audience and build trust.

Effective public communication requires active listening, empathy, and the ability to distill complex ideas into simple and relatable messages.

It involves leveraging various channels, such as social media, public speaking, and storytelling, to reach a wide range of individuals and communities.

By harnessing the power of public communication, leaders can inspire action, drive change, and create a collective vision for a better future.

Crisis Management

In the face of a crisis, effective crisis management is essential to navigate through challenges and ensure the resilience and success of an organization. When unexpected events occur, it's crucial to have a clear plan in place to address the situation promptly and efficiently.

Communication becomes paramount during crises, as it allows leaders to provide timely updates, reassure stakeholders, and offer guidance. Transparency and honesty are key in crisis management, as they build trust and credibility. Leaders should take charge, making quick decisions and taking swift action to mitigate the impact of the crisis.

This requires staying calm under pressure and rallying the team to work together towards a common goal. By being proactive and adaptable, leaders can navigate through the storm and emerge stronger on the other side.

Crisis management is not just about putting out fires; it's about finding opportunities for growth and innovation amidst adversity. It's an opportunity for leaders to demonstrate their true capabilities and showcase their ability to lead with resilience and determination.

So, in the face of a crisis, embrace the challenge, stay focused, and lead with confidence.

Community Leadership

In community leadership, volunteer management is crucial to effectively mobilize people to work towards a common goal. By engaging volunteers and providing them with meaningful opportunities, you can harness their skills and passion to make a difference in the community.

Additionally, community engagement is essential for fostering a sense of ownership and collective responsibility, as it encourages individuals to actively participate in decision-making processes and take action to address local issues.

Lastly, resource mobilization plays a key role in community leadership by identifying and securing the necessary resources, whether it's funding, materials, or expertise, to support and sustain community initiatives.

Volunteer Management

Though it may seem overwhelming, volunteer management is crucial for the success of any organization.

Studies have shown that volunteers are 27% more likely to donate financially to a cause they're passionate about. So, by effectively managing volunteers, you not only ensure the smooth running of your organization but also increase the chances of receiving financial support.

To effectively manage volunteers, it's essential to have a clear and well-defined volunteer program in place. This includes clearly outlining the roles and responsibilities of volunteers, providing them with proper training and support, and regularly communicating and acknowledging their contributions.

Additionally, it's important to establish strong relationships with volunteers by showing appreciation for their efforts and creating a positive and inclusive environment.

By implementing these practices, you can unleash the true power of volunteer leadership and create a thriving organization driven by passionate individuals working towards a common cause.

Community Engagement

Engaging with the community is an incredible opportunity to ignite passion and foster meaningful connections.

It allows you to tap into the collective power of individuals who share a common purpose and vision.

By actively involving the community, you can gain valuable insights, ideas, and support that can propel your leadership efforts forward.

Community engagement is not just about reaching out and getting people involved; it's about creating a sense of ownership and empowerment.

It's about listening to their needs, concerns, and aspirations, and working together to find solutions that benefit everyone.

When you engage with the community, you show that you value their input and are committed to making a positive impact.

It's a chance to build trust, build relationships, and build a stronger, more inclusive community.

So, don't underestimate the power of community engagement.

Embrace it, leverage it, and watch as it transforms your leadership journey into something truly extraordinary.

Resource Mobilization

Resource mobilization is a crucial aspect of effective leadership, as it enables you to tap into available resources and maximize their potential for impact.

For example, imagine a small community organization that successfully mobilizes volunteers and donations to build a much-needed playground for local children.

By effectively mobilizing resources, leaders can accomplish remarkable things that benefit their communities.

Whether it's securing funding, rallying support, or leveraging existing assets, resource mobilization allows leaders to overcome obstacles and achieve their goals.

It requires strategic thinking, effective communication, and strong relationship-building skills.

By harnessing the power of resource mobilization, leaders can make a tangible difference in the lives of those they serve.

Chapter 10: Transformational Leadership

In Chapter 10 of the book, you'll delve into the concept of Transformational Leadership. You'll gain a deep understanding of what it means to be a transformational leader and how it differs from other leadership styles.

Furthermore, you'll explore the significant impact that transformational leadership can have on individuals and organizations, inspiring positive change and growth.

Understanding Transformational Leadership

If you want to truly unleash the power of your leadership, it's important to understand the key points of vision creation, change implementation, and inspirational motivation.

Vision creation involves setting a clear and compelling direction for your team, inspiring them to strive for a common goal.

Change implementation requires the ability to effectively communicate and manage the process of change within your organization.

Finally, inspirational motivation is all about motivating and empowering your team members to go above and beyond, creating a positive and high-performing work environment.

Vision Creation

Imagine the exhilaration of creating a vision that ignites passion and propels your team towards a future filled with limitless possibilities. As a leader, your role in vision creation is crucial. It's not just about setting goals and objectives; it's about inspiring and motivating your team to believe in and work towards a shared purpose.

A compelling vision paints a vivid picture of what success looks like, providing a roadmap for everyone to follow. It allows your team to see beyond the present challenges and envision a better future. By involving your team in the vision creation process, you tap into their creativity and commitment, making them feel valued and empowered.

A well-crafted vision aligns individual goals with the larger organizational objectives, creating a sense of unity and cohesion. It becomes a driving force that guides decision-making, shapes strategies, and influences behaviors.

So, take the time to reflect on your organization's purpose, values, and aspirations, and craft a vision that captures the hearts and minds of your team. Inspire them to dream big, take risks, and work together towards a shared vision of success.

Change Implementation

Now that you've successfully created a compelling vision for your organization, it's time to tackle the next crucial step: change implementation.

Change can be a daunting process, but with the right approach, it can also be an opportunity for growth and transformation. As a leader, it's your responsibility to guide your team through this transition and ensure that the desired changes are effectively implemented.

This requires clear communication, stakeholder engagement, and a well-defined plan of action. By involving your team in the change process and providing them with the necessary support and resources, you can unleash their true potential and create a culture of continuous improvement.

Remember, change may be challenging, but it's also the catalyst for innovation and progress. Embrace it, and you'll be rewarded with a more resilient and adaptable organization.

Inspirational Motivation

Through your guidance and encouragement, you can ignite a spark within your team, inspiring them to reach new heights and overcome any obstacles that stand in their way.

As a leader, it's essential to provide your team with a clear vision and purpose, painting a picture of what success looks like and how it can be achieved. By setting high expectations and demonstrating your belief in their abilities, you can motivate your team members to push beyond their limits and strive for excellence.

Inspiring motivation goes beyond simply assigning tasks and giving orders; it involves creating a sense of enthusiasm and passion for the work at hand. By connecting with your team on a personal level and understanding their individual strengths and aspirations, you can tailor your approach to inspire and motivate each team member effectively.

Celebrate their successes, provide constructive feedback, and create a positive and supportive environment that encourages growth and innovation.

Remember, inspiration isn't a one-time event but a continuous process that requires consistent effort and genuine care for the development and well-being of your team.

By embodying the qualities of an inspiring leader, you can unlock the true potential of your team and lead them to achieve remarkable results.

Impact of Transformational Leadership

When it comes to the impact of transformational leadership, there are three key points to consider:

- Increased productivity: With transformational leaders at the helm, you can expect your team to be more motivated and driven, resulting in higher levels of productivity.

- Improved employee satisfaction: Employees under this type of leadership tend to feel more valued and supported, leading to greater job satisfaction.

- Enhanced innovation: The encouragement of creativity and out-of-the-box thinking by transformational leaders fosters a culture of innovation, propelling your organization forward.

Increased Productivity

By tapping into your true leadership potential, you can experience a significant boost in productivity, unleashing your full capabilities and achieving remarkable results.

When you embrace your role as a leader and inspire others to do the same, you create a culture of high performance and excellence.

Transformational leaders have the ability to motivate and empower their team members, fostering a sense of ownership and commitment.

By setting clear goals, providing support and resources, and encouraging continuous growth and development, you can create an environment where everyone is motivated to give their best.

As a result, productivity levels soar, and individuals are able to accomplish more than they ever thought possible.

When you lead with authenticity and passion, you inspire others to do the same, creating a ripple effect of increased productivity and success throughout the entire organization.

So, unleash your true leadership potential and watch as your productivity and the productivity of those around you reach new heights.

Improved Employee Satisfaction

Boost your team's morale and watch as their satisfaction levels skyrocket, creating a positive work environment that is as refreshing as a breath of fresh air.

When employees feel satisfied, they're more engaged, motivated, and productive. They're invested in their work and more likely to go the extra mile to achieve success.

Improved employee satisfaction also leads to higher retention rates, as happy employees are less likely to seek opportunities elsewhere.

By focusing on improving employee satisfaction, you can create a culture of collaboration, trust, and respect. Provide opportunities for growth and development, recognize and appreciate their contributions, and create a work-life balance that promotes well-being.

By doing so, you can unleash the true power of leadership and create a workplace where everyone thrives.

Enhanced Innovation

Now that you've improved employee satisfaction within your organization, it's time to focus on enhancing innovation.

By creating a work environment that encourages new ideas and creative thinking, you can unlock the true potential of your team.

Innovation is the key to staying ahead in today's fast-paced and ever-changing business world. It allows you to develop unique products or services, streamline processes, and find new ways to solve problems.

By fostering a culture of innovation, you empower your employees to think outside the box and take risks. This not only leads to groundbreaking ideas but also boosts employee engagement and satisfaction.

Encourage collaboration, provide resources for experimentation, and celebrate failures as learning opportunities.

By embracing innovation, you'll unleash the true power of your team and drive your organization towards future success.

Chapter 11: Leadership and Culture

In this chapter, you'll explore the importance of culture-driven leadership and how it can shape the success of an organization.

You'll learn strategies for building a positive organizational culture that fosters collaboration, innovation, and employee engagement.

Additionally, you'll gain insights on how inclusivity and respect play a crucial role in effective leadership, creating a welcoming and inclusive environment for all team members.

Culture-Driven Leadership

When it comes to culture-driven leadership, it's important to understand how culture is defined and its impact on leadership style.

Culture shapes the beliefs, values, and behaviors of a group, which in turn influence how leaders approach their roles.

By recognizing the connection between culture and leadership, you can enhance your effectiveness as a leader by adapting your style to align with the cultural norms and expectations of your team.

Culture Defined

Amidst the vibrant tapestry of an organization, culture weaves its invisible threads, shaping the collective identity and driving the pulse of its people.

Culture is not just a buzzword, but a powerful force that influences how individuals behave, make decisions, and interact with one another.

It encompasses the shared values, beliefs, and assumptions that guide the actions and attitudes within an organization.

A strong culture creates a sense of belonging and purpose, fostering employee engagement, satisfaction, and loyalty.

It sets the tone for how things are done and what is considered acceptable or unacceptable.

Understanding and defining the culture of an organization is essential for effective leadership.

It enables leaders to align their actions and decisions with the values and beliefs of the organization, creating a harmonious and productive work environment.

By nurturing a positive culture, leaders can unleash the true power of their teams, leading to increased collaboration, innovation, and ultimately, organizational success.

The Impact of Culture on Leadership Style

Imagine yourself as a leader, navigating the currents of organizational culture and witnessing how it shapes your leadership style. Culture has a profound impact on how leaders approach their roles and interact with their teams. It influences the way decisions are made, communication is conducted, and goals are pursued.

A culture that values collaboration and open communication will likely foster a leadership style that is inclusive and transparent. On the other hand, a culture that prioritizes hierarchy and control may lead to a leadership style that is more authoritative and directive.

Understanding the impact of culture on your leadership style allows you to adapt and align your approach to best suit the needs of your organization and team. By acknowledging the influence of culture, you can harness its power to create a positive and effective leadership style that inspires and empowers others.

Culture and Leadership Effectiveness

Now that you understand the influence of culture on leadership style, let's dive deeper into the concept of culture and its impact on leadership effectiveness.

Culture plays a crucial role in shaping the way leaders lead and how their actions are perceived by their team members. Effective leaders understand the importance of aligning their leadership style with the cultural values and norms of their organization or team. By doing so, they can build stronger relationships, foster trust, and create a positive work environment.

Moreover, leaders who are culturally aware and adaptable can navigate through diverse perspectives and leverage the strengths of their team members from different cultural backgrounds. This not only enhances their leadership effectiveness but also promotes innovation and creativity within the organization.

Therefore, it is essential for leaders to recognize the significance of culture and actively incorporate it into their leadership approach to unleash their true power and drive outstanding results.

Building a Positive Organizational Culture

In order to build a positive organizational culture, it's essential for leaders to take an active role. They must lead by example and consistently demonstrate the values and behaviors they want to foster within the organization.

By focusing on core values and encouraging positive interactions, leaders can create a culture that promotes collaboration, growth, and success.

Role of Leadership in Culture Building

Embedded within the fabric of an organization, leadership exudes a magnetic influence that shapes the very essence of its culture. As a leader, you hold the power to create a positive and thriving work environment. Your actions, decisions, and behaviors set the tone for how employees interact, collaborate, and engage with one another.

By embodying the values and principles that you want to see reflected in your organization, you can inspire others to do the same. Your ability to communicate effectively, delegate tasks, and provide guidance and support plays a crucial role in fostering a culture of trust, respect, and accountability.

It is through your leadership that you can establish a shared vision, align goals, and motivate your team to reach new heights. By being intentional in your efforts to build a positive organizational culture, you empower your employees to be their best selves and contribute to the overall success of the organization.

Fostering Core Values

Building a positive organizational culture begins by fostering core values that guide you and your colleagues in your actions and decision-making, ultimately leading to increased productivity and employee satisfaction.

Did you know that companies with strong cultures have a 4x higher employee engagement rate?

By clearly defining and promoting core values such as integrity, respect, and teamwork, you create a shared understanding of what behaviors are expected and encouraged within the organization. These values serve as a compass, guiding you and your team in making ethical choices and building strong relationships.

When everyone is aligned with these core values, it creates a sense of purpose and unity, leading to a more positive work environment.

Furthermore, fostering core values helps to attract and retain top talent, as employees are more likely to be drawn to organizations that align with their own personal values.

Ultimately, by investing in and nurturing core values, you lay the foundation for a thriving and successful organizational culture.

Encouraging Positive Interactions

Encourage positive interactions by fostering a supportive and collaborative work environment where you can connect with your colleagues and build strong relationships.

Creating an atmosphere where individuals feel valued and respected is essential for promoting positive interactions.

Encourage open communication and active listening to ensure that everyone's ideas and opinions are heard.

Foster a sense of teamwork by promoting collaboration and highlighting the importance of each team member's unique contributions.

By creating opportunities for social interactions, such as team-building activities or informal gatherings, you can facilitate the development of strong relationships among colleagues.

Encouraging positive interactions not only boosts morale and productivity but also creates a sense of belonging and camaraderie within the team.

Inclusivity and Respect in Leadership

When it comes to effective leadership, leading with respect is paramount.

By treating others with dignity and acknowledging their worth, you create an inclusive environment where all team members feel valued and empowered.

Promoting inclusion goes hand in hand with respect, as it involves actively seeking out diverse perspectives and ensuring that everyone has a voice at the table.

Leading with Respect

Imagine if you could lead with respect and create an environment where every team member feels valued and appreciated for their unique contributions. Leading with respect means treating others with dignity, listening to their ideas, and acknowledging their expertise.

It means creating a safe space for open and honest communication, where diverse perspectives are welcomed and embraced. When you lead with respect, you inspire trust and loyalty among your team members, fostering a sense of belonging and empowerment.

By recognizing and appreciating the strengths of each individual, you can harness the true power of your team and create a culture of collaboration and innovation. So, make an effort to actively listen, show empathy, and demonstrate appreciation for the diverse talents and experiences that each team member brings to the table.

Leading with respect not only enhances productivity and performance but also cultivates a positive and inclusive work environment where everyone can thrive.

Promoting Inclusion

Creating an inclusive environment allows individuals to feel valued and appreciated for their unique perspectives and experiences. It's essential for leaders to promote inclusion within their organizations as it fosters collaboration, innovation, and creativity. By embracing diversity and creating a sense of belonging, leaders can unlock the full potential of their teams.

Inclusion is not just about inviting different voices to the table; it also involves actively listening, acknowledging, and respecting those voices. Leaders can promote inclusion by encouraging open communication, creating opportunities for diverse perspectives to be heard, and fostering an environment where everyone feels comfortable expressing their ideas and opinions.

Additionally, leaders can provide training and resources to help individuals understand and appreciate different cultures, backgrounds, and experiences. By doing so, they can create a workplace that celebrates diversity and empowers individuals to bring their whole selves to work, which ultimately leads to increased employee engagement, satisfaction, and productivity.

Chapter 12: Leaders as Mentors

In Chapter 12, you'll explore the role of mentoring in leadership and how it can unleash the true power of leaders.

You'll learn about effective mentoring techniques that can help you develop and guide your team members.

Additionally, you'll discover how to encourage a mentoring culture within your organization, fostering growth, collaboration, and personal development.

Role of Mentoring in Leadership

If you want to unleash the true power of your leadership, mentoring plays a crucial role. By nurturing talent, you not only help individuals reach their full potential, but also create a strong team that can achieve extraordinary results.

Sharing knowledge allows you to pass on valuable insights and skills, empowering others to excel in their roles.

Lastly, providing guidance gives your mentees the support and direction they need to navigate challenges and grow as leaders themselves.

Remember, by investing in mentoring, you not only benefit others, but also enhance your own leadership abilities.

Nurturing Talent

You think you're nurturing talent, but really you're just creating a bunch of entitled, self-absorbed prima donnas who think they're God's gift to the world.

True talent nurturing goes beyond simply giving praise and recognition for good performance. It requires a delicate balance of challenge and support, pushing individuals to reach their full potential while providing the guidance and resources they need to succeed.

Nurturing talent means creating an environment where individuals feel empowered to take risks, make mistakes, and learn from them. It means providing opportunities for growth and development, whether through formal training programs or on-the-job experiences. It means fostering a culture of continuous learning and improvement, where feedback is not only welcomed but actively sought after.

As a leader, it's your responsibility to identify and cultivate talent within your team, but it's equally important to ensure that this talent is being nurtured in a way that encourages humility, collaboration, and a commitment to the greater good. It's about helping individuals understand that their success isn't measured solely by their own accomplishments, but by the collective achievements of the team.

So, next time you think you're nurturing talent, take a step back and ask yourself if you're truly fostering an environment that cultivates the kind of talent that'll make a lasting impact.

Sharing Knowledge

Imagine the incredible impact you could have by generously sharing your knowledge and wisdom with others, creating a ripple effect of growth and innovation throughout your team and beyond.

When you share your knowledge, you empower others to learn and grow, enabling them to reach their full potential.

By openly sharing your expertise, you not only contribute to the development of your team members but also foster a culture of collaboration and continuous learning.

Sharing knowledge also allows for the exchange of ideas and perspectives, sparking creativity and innovation.

As a leader, it's essential to recognize that your knowledge is a valuable resource that can be leveraged to drive positive change and inspire others.

So, take the initiative to share your knowledge through mentoring, training sessions, or simply by being open and approachable.

Embrace the opportunity to be a catalyst for growth and transformation, and watch as your team and organization flourish.

Providing Guidance

With the power of knowledge shared, you have the ability to act as a guiding light for your team members, illuminating the path forward and fostering growth and development. As a leader, it's your responsibility to provide guidance and direction to those you lead.

By offering your expertise and experience, you can help your team members navigate challenges, make informed decisions, and achieve their goals. Providing guidance means taking the time to listen to your team members, understand their needs and aspirations, and then offering them the support and advice they require.

It means being accessible and approachable, creating an environment where individuals feel comfortable seeking guidance and asking for help. By being a source of guidance, you not only empower your team members to take ownership of their work but also enable them to reach their full potential.

So, embrace the power of knowledge and use it to guide and empower those around you.

Mentoring Techniques for Leaders

When it comes to mentoring techniques for leaders, there are three key points to keep in mind:

– Active listening: It's important to actively listen to your mentees, providing them with your full attention and making them feel heard and valued.

– Giving constructive feedback: Offering constructive feedback in a supportive and helpful manner can greatly contribute to their growth and development.

– Setting goals: Lastly, setting clear and achievable goals with your mentees will not only help them stay focused and motivated, but also provide a roadmap for their success.

Active Listening

Engaging in active listening allows you, as a leader, to truly understand and connect with your team members. It goes beyond simply hearing what they're saying; it involves fully focusing on them, showing genuine interest, and providing your undivided attention.

Through active listening, you create a safe space for your team members to express their thoughts, ideas, and concerns, which can lead to increased trust and collaboration. By actively listening, you gain valuable insights into their perspectives, needs, and motivations, enabling you to make more informed decisions that benefit both the individual and the team as a whole.

Active listening also helps you to identify any potential misunderstandings or miscommunications, allowing you to address them promptly and effectively. Ultimately, by practicing active listening, you demonstrate respect, empathy, and a willingness to learn from others, which can foster a positive and productive work environment.

Giving Constructive Feedback

Giving constructive feedback involves actively listening to your team members and providing specific examples of their strengths and areas for improvement. It also involves offering guidance on how they can enhance their performance. By actively listening, you show your team members that you value their opinions and perspectives, which can foster a sense of trust and collaboration.

When giving feedback, it's important to be specific and provide examples so that your team members can understand exactly what you're referring to. This helps them to see both their strengths and areas for improvement more clearly. Additionally, offering guidance on how they can enhance their performance shows that you're invested in their growth and development. By providing practical suggestions and actionable steps, you can empower your team members to take ownership of their own improvement and achieve better results.

When done effectively, giving constructive feedback can not only improve individual performance but also contribute to the overall success of the team.

Setting Goals

Setting goals helps to create a clear path for success and motivates team members to strive for growth and achievement. By setting specific and measurable goals, individuals are able to focus their efforts on what needs to be accomplished, allowing them to stay organized and prioritize their tasks effectively.

Moreover, setting goals provides a sense of direction and purpose, as it outlines the desired outcome and the steps required to reach it. This clarity not only helps team members understand what is expected of them, but also allows them to track their progress and celebrate milestones along the way.

Additionally, setting goals promotes accountability, as team members become responsible for their own performance and are motivated to push themselves beyond their comfort zones. It encourages them to continuously improve their skills and knowledge, fostering a growth mindset within the team.

Overall, goal setting is a powerful tool that not only enhances individual performance but also drives team success by aligning everyone towards a common vision and fueling their determination to achieve it.

Encouraging a Mentoring Culture

To encourage a mentoring culture, you need to focus on three key points.

First, train your leaders to become effective mentors by providing them with the necessary skills and knowledge. This will help them guide and support their mentees in the most impactful way.

Second, support the mentoring relationships by creating a conducive environment where both mentors and mentees feel empowered and motivated. This can be done through regular check-ins, providing resources, and facilitating networking opportunities.

Lastly, recognize and celebrate mentoring success by acknowledging the achievements and growth of both mentors and mentees. This will not only boost their confidence but also inspire others to participate in the mentoring culture.

Training Leaders to Mentor

You gotta admit, training leaders to mentor is like teaching a fish to swim - it's like telling a bird how to fly. It may seem redundant and unnecessary, but the truth is, even the most accomplished leaders can benefit from learning how to effectively mentor others.

Mentoring is not just about imparting knowledge or providing guidance; it is about building strong relationships and fostering growth. By training leaders to mentor, organizations can create a culture of continuous learning and development, where employees feel supported and empowered to reach their full potential.

Effective mentoring requires skills such as active listening, asking powerful questions, and providing constructive feedback. Through training, leaders can learn these skills and understand the importance of creating a safe and trusting environment for their mentees. They can also learn how to tailor their mentoring approach to meet the unique needs and goals of each individual.

Ultimately, training leaders to mentor is an investment in the future success of both the leaders themselves and the organization as a whole. It enables leaders to not only lead, but also inspire and empower others to become leaders themselves.

Supporting Mentoring Relationships

Engage in the process of supporting mentoring relationships by providing resources and guidance to ensure both mentors and mentees thrive and grow.

As a leader, it's crucial to recognize the importance of supporting these relationships and the impact they can have on individual development and organizational success.

By offering resources such as training materials, workshops, and access to relevant networks, you can equip mentors with the necessary skills and knowledge to effectively guide and support their mentees.

Additionally, providing guidance and regular check-ins can help mentors navigate any challenges they may encounter and ensure they're on the right track.

It's equally important to support mentees by offering them opportunities for growth and development, such as providing access to learning resources, connecting them with mentors from different backgrounds, and encouraging them to set goals and take ownership of their own learning journey.

By actively engaging in this process, you can create a culture of support and growth where both mentors and mentees can thrive and reach their full potential.

Recognizing Mentoring Success

Recognizing mentoring success is like uncovering a hidden gem, as it reveals the incredible impact and growth that can be achieved through effective mentorship. When you take the time to acknowledge and celebrate the achievements of your mentees, you not only boost their confidence and motivation, but also inspire them to continue striving for excellence.

By highlighting their accomplishments, you provide them with a sense of validation and recognition, which can be a powerful driving force for their personal and professional development. Recognizing mentoring success also serves as a reminder of the significant role you play as a mentor, as you witness firsthand the positive outcomes of your guidance and support.

It reinforces the importance of your role and encourages you to continue investing your time and energy into nurturing the talents and potential of your mentees. So, don't underestimate the value of recognizing mentoring success. It can truly make a difference in the lives of your mentees and strengthen the bond between mentor and mentee.

Chapter 13: Female Leadership

In this chapter, you'll explore the importance of understanding female leadership and the ways it can be promoted.

Understanding female leadership involves recognizing the unique strengths and perspectives that women bring to the table. It also involves understanding how these strengths and perspectives can positively impact organizations.

By promoting female leadership, organizations not only create more inclusive and diverse environments, but they also tap into a wealth of untapped talent and potential.

Understanding Female Leadership

If you want to understand the true power of female leadership, you need to look beyond authority and explore the characteristics that make these leaders unique.

Female leaders often possess qualities such as empathy, collaboration, and intuition, which enable them to inspire and motivate their teams.

However, it's important to recognize that female leaders also face unique challenges, such as gender bias and the need to prove themselves in male-dominated industries.

Despite these obstacles, female leaders have achieved remarkable accomplishments, breaking glass ceilings and paving the way for future generations of women in leadership roles.

Characteristics of Female Leaders

Imagine yourself in a room filled with powerful leaders, and you can't help but notice the remarkable characteristics that set female leaders apart from the rest. They possess a unique ability to empathize and connect with others on a deeper level, which enables them to build strong relationships and foster collaboration within their teams.

Female leaders also tend to be great communicators, effectively conveying their ideas and inspiring others to take action. They excel at multitasking and problem-solving, effortlessly juggling multiple responsibilities and finding innovative solutions to complex issues.

Additionally, female leaders often demonstrate a high level of emotional intelligence, allowing them to navigate challenging situations with grace and resilience. They are inclusive and value diverse perspectives, creating a sense of belonging and empowerment among their team members.

Female leaders are not afraid to take risks and challenge the status quo, pushing boundaries and driving positive change. Overall, their unique blend of empathy, communication skills, multitasking abilities, emotional intelligence, inclusivity, and courage make them exceptional leaders who can truly unleash the true power of leadership.

Challenges Faced by Female Leaders

Picture yourself as a female leader, facing an onslaught of seemingly insurmountable challenges that threaten to crush your spirit and hinder your progress towards success.

As a female leader, you may find yourself constantly battling against gender biases and stereotypes that question your ability to lead effectively. The pressure to prove yourself worthy can be overwhelming, and it often feels like you are fighting an uphill battle.

Additionally, the lack of representation and support from other female leaders can make you feel isolated and alone in your journey.

Balancing work and family responsibilities can be another major challenge, as societal expectations still place a disproportionate burden on women.

However, despite these obstacles, it's important to remember that you possess the strength, resilience, and determination to overcome them.

Seek out mentors and allies who can provide guidance and support, and don't be afraid to speak up and assert your worth.

By staying true to your values, embracing your unique perspective, and advocating for change, you can break through these barriers and unleash your true power as a female leader.

Achievements by Female Leaders

As a female leader, you've conquered countless obstacles and shattered glass ceilings, leaving an indelible mark on history. Your achievements are nothing short of extraordinary.

You've risen to the top of your profession, breaking through barriers and paving the way for future generations of women. Your leadership has inspired others and challenged the status quo. You've proven that gender isn't a limitation, but rather a source of strength and innovation.

Your accomplishments have not only advanced your own career but have also created opportunities for others. You've mentored and empowered countless individuals, helping them reach their full potential.

Your ability to navigate complex situations, make tough decisions, and lead with empathy and compassion is truly remarkable. Your achievements as a female leader serve as a powerful reminder that anything is possible with determination, resilience, and a vision for change.

Your impact extends far beyond the boardroom - it reaches into the hearts and minds of those who've been inspired by your leadership. Keep pushing boundaries, challenging norms, and unleashing the true power of leadership.

Your journey isn't over, and the world eagerly awaits the next chapter of your remarkable story.

Promoting Female Leadership

To promote female leadership, it's crucial to encourage diversity within organizations by creating an inclusive environment that values and celebrates different perspectives.

Women leadership development programs can be instrumental in providing women with the necessary skills, knowledge, and support to thrive in leadership roles.

Additionally, recognizing and rewarding female leaders for their achievements can help inspire and motivate other women to pursue leadership positions.

Encouraging Diversity

Imagine a workplace where every voice is valued and every perspective is celebrated, creating a vibrant tapestry of diversity that fuels innovation and fosters a culture of inclusivity.

Encouraging diversity not only brings together people from different backgrounds, experiences, and beliefs, but it also allows for a wider range of ideas and solutions to be considered.

When individuals from diverse backgrounds collaborate, they bring unique insights and alternative ways of thinking, challenging the status quo and pushing the boundaries of what is possible.

This diversity of thought and perspective can lead to breakthrough innovations and creative problem-solving that may not have been achieved in a more homogenous environment.

Moreover, promoting diversity sends a powerful message to employees and potential recruits that the organization values and respects differences, creating a sense of belonging and attracting top talent.

By embracing diversity, companies can tap into the true power of leadership, leveraging the strengths and talents of all individuals to drive success and create a more inclusive and equitable workplace.

Women Leadership Development Programs

Now that we've explored the importance of encouraging diversity in leadership, let's dive into the realm of women's leadership development programs.

These programs are specifically designed to empower and equip women with the skills, knowledge, and support needed to excel in leadership roles.

By addressing the unique challenges and barriers faced by women in the workplace, these programs aim to bridge the gender gap and create a more inclusive and diverse leadership landscape.

Through mentorship, training, networking opportunities, and skill-building workshops, women's leadership development programs provide a platform for women to unleash their true potential and make their mark as influential leaders.

By investing in these programs, organizations not only foster gender equality but also tap into a vast pool of talent and perspectives, resulting in better decision-making, increased innovation, and overall organizational success.

Recognizing and Rewarding Female Leaders

Recognizing and rewarding female leaders is not just a matter of fairness, but it's also a strategic move for organizations to harness the immense potential and unique perspectives that women bring to the table.

By acknowledging and celebrating the achievements of female leaders, organizations can create a culture that values diversity and inclusion, which in turn leads to increased innovation and better decision-making.

When female leaders are recognized and rewarded for their contributions, it sends a powerful message to other women within the organization that their voices and talents are valued, inspiring them to aspire to leadership roles.

Additionally, recognizing and rewarding female leaders can help break down gender stereotypes and biases, challenging the traditional notion of leadership and paving the way for more women to rise to the top.

Organizations that actively recognize and reward female leaders not only benefit from their individual skills and abilities, but also from the positive impact it has on their overall organizational culture and success.

Chapter 14: Leadership Failures

In Chapter 14, you'll delve into the topic of Leadership Failures. This chapter emphasizes the importance of understanding leadership failures. It allows you to identify the underlying causes and patterns. By preventing leadership failures, you can create a more successful and effective leadership style.

Finally, learning from failures is crucial for personal and professional growth. It enables you to make better decisions and avoid repeating past mistakes.

Understanding Leadership Failures

Do you ever wonder why some leaders fail to achieve their goals and make a positive impact?

Well, there are several causes of leadership failures that can hinder their effectiveness. These can range from a lack of self-awareness and emotional intelligence to poor communication and decision-making skills.

The impact of these failures can be significant, affecting not only the leader's own performance but also the morale and productivity of their team.

To illustrate, some examples of leadership failures include Volkswagen's emission scandal and the downfall of companies like Enron and Lehman Brothers.

By understanding these causes, impacts, and examples of leadership failures, you can learn valuable lessons on how to avoid them and become a more successful leader.

Causes of Leadership Failures

Despite your best efforts, you often find yourself grappling with the enigmatic causes of your failures, as if trapped in a labyrinth of your own making.

Leadership failures can stem from a multitude of factors, each contributing to the overall breakdown of effectiveness.

One common cause is a lack of self-awareness, which prevents leaders from recognizing their own weaknesses and blind spots.

Additionally, poor communication skills can lead to misunderstandings, conflicts, and a breakdown in trust within the team.

Another cause of leadership failures is the inability to adapt to changing circumstances and embrace innovation.

Leaders who resist change and cling to outdated methods often find themselves left behind in a rapidly evolving world.

Lastly, a lack of empathy and emotional intelligence can hinder a leader's ability to connect with and inspire their team members.

By understanding these causes of leadership failures, you can begin to address them and unleash the true power of your leadership.

Impact of Leadership Failures

Leadership failures can have a profound and devastating impact on teams, causing a breakdown of trust, demotivation, and a sense of hopelessness.

When leaders fail to effectively guide and inspire their teams, it creates an atmosphere of uncertainty and doubt. Employees may lose faith in the direction of the organization and feel disengaged from their work. This lack of trust can lead to decreased productivity, as team members may become hesitant to take risks or put in extra effort.

Additionally, leadership failures can demotivate employees, as they may feel undervalued or unsupported. Without proper guidance and encouragement, individuals may struggle to find meaning and purpose in their work, leading to decreased job satisfaction and increased turnover.

Furthermore, leadership failures can instill a sense of hopelessness within teams. When employees witness their leaders making poor decisions or acting in unethical ways, it can erode their belief in the organization's ability to succeed. This can create a toxic work environment where innovation and collaboration are stifled.

In summary, the impact of leadership failures is far-reaching and detrimental, affecting team dynamics, employee morale, and overall organizational performance. It's crucial for leaders to recognize the consequences of their actions and strive to improve their leadership skills to avoid these negative outcomes.

Examples of Leadership Failures

One prime example of a leadership failure is when a manager turned a blind eye to the unethical practices happening within the company, allowing corruption to spread like wildfire throughout the organization. This failure of leadership not only undermines the trust and morale of the employees, but it also tarnishes the company's reputation and can lead to severe legal and financial consequences.

When leaders fail to address unethical behavior, they send a message that it's acceptable and even encouraged within the organization. This lack of accountability creates a toxic work environment where employees feel unsupported and undervalued.

It's crucial for leaders to set a strong ethical tone, enforce policies, and hold individuals accountable for their actions. By doing so, they can prevent the devastating consequences of leadership failures and foster a culture of integrity and trust within the organization.

Preventing Leadership Failures

To prevent leadership failures, it's crucial to continually develop your skills. This means actively seeking out opportunities to learn and grow, whether through workshops, courses, or mentoring.

Additionally, seeking feedback from others is essential to identify blind spots and areas for improvement.

Lastly, maintaining high ethical standards is key to building trust and credibility as a leader. Always strive to do what's right, even when faced with difficult decisions or pressures.

Continual Skill Development

Improve your leadership skills by constantly developing and honing your abilities. In order to be an effective leader, it's crucial to continuously learn and grow.

This means seeking out opportunities for skill development, whether it's through workshops, seminars, or even reading books on leadership.

By investing time and effort into expanding your knowledge and improving your skills, you'll be better equipped to navigate the challenges of leadership.

Additionally, it's important to actively practice and apply what you've learned in real-life situations. This allows you to refine your abilities and adapt to different circumstances.

Remember, leadership isn't a static concept, but rather a dynamic process that requires continuous improvement. So, make it a priority to continually develop your skills and unleash your true power as a leader.

Seeking Feedback

Seeking feedback is like opening Pandora's box of self-discovery, where you uncover hidden gems of insight and unlock your potential as a leader.

When you actively seek feedback from those around you, you open yourself up to a wealth of knowledge and perspectives that can help you grow and develop as a leader.

Feedback allows you to understand how your actions and decisions are perceived by others, giving you the opportunity to make necessary adjustments and improvements. It provides valuable insights into your strengths and weaknesses, enabling you to leverage your strengths and work on areas that need improvement.

Seeking feedback also demonstrates your willingness to learn and grow, which can inspire trust and respect from your team.

By embracing feedback, you create an environment where open communication and continuous improvement are valued, leading to increased collaboration and innovation within your team.

So, don't shy away from seeking feedback; instead, embrace it as a powerful tool for personal and professional growth.

Maintaining Ethical Standards

Maintaining ethical standards is an essential aspect of leadership, as it requires you to consistently uphold principles and values that guide your actions and decisions.

As a leader, you have the power to influence and impact those around you, and maintaining ethical standards ensures that your influence is positive and beneficial.

Ethical leadership involves being transparent, accountable, and fair in your interactions with others. It means treating everyone with respect and dignity, regardless of their position or background.

By setting a high ethical standard, you inspire trust and loyalty among your team members, fostering a positive work environment where everyone feels valued and respected.

When faced with difficult decisions, ethical leaders consider the impact on all stakeholders and choose the course of action that aligns with their values and principles. They prioritize doing the right thing over personal gain or short-term success.

By maintaining ethical standards, you not only demonstrate integrity and authenticity, but you also create a culture of ethical behavior within your organization, setting the stage for long-term success and positive impact.

Learning from Failures

When it comes to learning from failures, reflecting on your mistakes is crucial. Taking the time to analyze what went wrong and why can provide valuable insights for improvement.

Additionally, rebuilding trust is essential after a failure, as it allows you to regain credibility and move forward.

Finally, implementing changes based on the lessons learned from failures is key to preventing similar mistakes in the future and ensuring growth and success.

Reflecting on Mistakes

Despite our best intentions, sometimes we stumble and fall, but it's through these mistakes that we can truly grow and evolve as leaders, like a phoenix rising from the ashes.

Reflecting on our mistakes allows us to gain valuable insights into our own strengths and weaknesses, enabling us to make better decisions in the future. It's in these moments of self-reflection that we uncover hidden patterns and behaviors that may have contributed to our missteps.

By acknowledging and owning our mistakes, we demonstrate humility and authenticity, which in turn fosters trust and respect from our team. Reflecting on mistakes also helps us identify areas for improvement and develop strategies to prevent similar errors in the future.

It's through this process of continuous learning and growth that we unleash the true power of leadership, allowing us to inspire and motivate others to reach their full potential.

So, the next time you stumble, don't shy away from reflecting on your mistakes; embrace them as opportunities for growth and watch yourself rise to new heights as a leader.

Rebuilding Trust

Embrace the challenge of rebuilding trust by demonstrating consistent and reliable behavior and fostering open communication. Actively address the concerns and doubts of your team members. Trust is a fragile thing, and once it's broken, it takes time and effort to rebuild. Start by consistently following through on your commitments and being transparent in your actions. Show your team that they can rely on you and that you're dedicated to their success.

Additionally, create an environment of open communication where everyone feels comfortable expressing their concerns and doubts. Be receptive to feedback and actively work towards resolving any issues that arise. By taking these steps, you can rebuild trust and create a stronger and more cohesive team.

Implementing Changes

Now that you've successfully rebuilt trust within your team, it's time to move on to the next crucial step: implementing changes.

As a leader, you possess the power to drive transformation and inspire your team to embrace new ways of doing things. This process requires a proactive approach. You actively involve your team members in the decision-making process and communicate the reasons behind the changes. By doing so, you empower them to take ownership of the changes and align their actions accordingly.

Remember, change can be uncomfortable for some individuals, so it's essential to provide support and guidance throughout the implementation process. Emphasize the benefits of the changes and how they align with the team's goals and overall vision.

By effectively implementing changes, you create an environment that fosters growth, innovation, and continuous improvement.

Chapter 15: Adaptive Leadership

In Chapter 15, you'll delve into the world of adaptive leadership. This subtopic focuses on defining adaptive leadership. It also explores the essential skills required for adaptive leaders. In addition, it helps you understand how to effectively implement adaptive leadership strategies. By understanding and practicing adaptive leadership, you'll be equipped with the tools to navigate the complex and ever-changing landscape of leadership with confidence and success.

Defining Adaptive Leadership

In this discussion, you'll explore the concept of adaptability and its significance in effective leadership. You'll learn about the Adaptive Leadership Model, which goes beyond traditional authority and focuses on unleashing the true power of leadership.

Additionally, you'll examine the role of adaptive leadership in change management and how it can help navigate and drive successful organizational transformations.

Understanding Adaptability

Imagine how much more effective you could be as a leader if you embraced adaptability, a quality that research shows is possessed by only 27% of managers.

Being adaptable means having the ability to adjust and thrive in the face of change and uncertainty. It means being open to new ideas, approaches, and perspectives. By being adaptable, you can effectively navigate through challenging situations, make informed decisions, and inspire your team to do the same.

Adaptability allows you to quickly assess and respond to unexpected circumstances, capitalize on emerging opportunities, and stay ahead of the competition. It also fosters a culture of innovation and continuous improvement within your organization.

So, how can you develop and enhance your adaptability as a leader? Start by embracing a growth mindset and being open to learning. Seek feedback and actively listen to others' perspectives. Be willing to step outside of your comfort zone and take calculated risks. Cultivate a sense of curiosity and stay abreast of current trends and developments in your industry.

Remember, adaptability is not just a desirable trait for leaders; it is an essential skill that can unlock your true potential and enable you to lead with confidence and success.

Adaptive Leadership Model

The Adaptive Leadership Model offers a framework for you to effectively navigate and thrive in dynamic and uncertain environments. It acknowledges that leadership is not just about authority and control, but about being adaptable and responsive to the ever-changing needs of your team and organization.

This model encourages you to not only identify the challenges and opportunities that arise, but also to understand the underlying values and motivations of your team members. By doing so, you can effectively mobilize and empower them to take ownership of the problem-solving process.

The Adaptive Leadership Model emphasizes the importance of experimentation and learning, encouraging you to test and refine your strategies as you go along. It recognizes that leadership is a continuous process of adaptation and growth, and provides you with the tools and mindset to effectively lead in today's complex and uncertain world.

Role of Adaptive Leadership in Change Management

Now that you have a good understanding of the Adaptive Leadership Model, let's dive into the role it plays in change management.

Change is inevitable in any organization, and being able to effectively lead and manage that change is crucial.

Adaptive leadership provides a framework that empowers leaders to navigate through the complexities of change. It encourages leaders to embrace uncertainty, challenge the status quo, and mobilize others to adapt and thrive in the face of change.

By focusing on the needs of the organization and its people, adaptive leadership enables leaders to identify the necessary changes, build trust, and create a shared vision that inspires and motivates others to embrace the change.

Through its practical and insightful approach, adaptive leadership equips leaders with the tools and mindset to successfully lead change and unleash the true power of leadership.

Skills for Adaptive Leaders

When it comes to being an adaptive leader, there are several key skills that you need to possess.

Problem-solving is essential, as you'll often be faced with complex challenges that require innovative solutions.

Handling ambiguity is also crucial, as you'll need to navigate uncertain situations with confidence and clarity.

Additionally, your ability to influence and negotiate will play a significant role in driving change and achieving desired outcomes.

Problem-Solving

Imagine yourself as a fearless captain navigating through treacherous waters of uncertainty, effortlessly steering your team towards innovative solutions. As a leader, problem-solving is a crucial skill that allows you to tackle challenges head-on and find effective resolutions.

The ability to identify problems, analyze them, and generate creative solutions is what sets adaptive leaders apart. By fostering a culture of open communication and collaboration, you empower your team members to contribute their unique perspectives and insights, collectively enhancing problem-solving capabilities.

Effective problem-solving involves breaking down complex issues into manageable parts, considering multiple perspectives, and thinking outside the box to uncover innovative solutions. As a leader, it's important to encourage experimentation, embrace failure as a learning opportunity, and celebrate successes.

By mastering the art of problem-solving, you unleash the true power of leadership, driving your team towards success in the face of uncertainty.

Handling Ambiguity

Handling ambiguity is a skill that allows you, as a leader, to navigate through uncertain situations with confidence, embracing the unknown and adapting to change.

Ambiguity is a constant in today's fast-paced and ever-changing business world, and leaders who can effectively handle it have a significant advantage.

When faced with ambiguity, it's important to remain calm and composed, and not let the uncertainty paralyze you. Instead, embrace the opportunity to think creatively and explore different options.

Look for patterns and trends, and use your intuition to make informed decisions. Additionally, be open to feedback and input from others, as their perspectives can provide valuable insights.

Finally, be flexible and adaptable, willing to change course if necessary. By mastering the skill of handling ambiguity, you can lead your team through uncertain times and come out stronger on the other side.

Influence and Negotiation

Influence and negotiation are essential skills for leaders to effectively navigate and shape outcomes. As a leader, you must understand that your ability to influence and negotiate can greatly impact the success of your team and organization. By mastering these skills, you can build strong relationships, gain support for your ideas, and drive positive change.

Influence is about inspiring and persuading others to take action, while negotiation involves finding common ground and reaching mutually beneficial agreements. To be successful in these areas, it's important to listen actively, understand the needs and motivations of others, and communicate your ideas effectively.

By leveraging your influence and negotiation skills, you can lead your team towards achieving shared goals and overcoming challenges.

Implementing Adaptive Leadership

When implementing adaptive leadership, you'll need to address complex challenges head-on. This means embracing the uncertainty and ambiguity that comes with navigating through difficult situations.

Additionally, it's crucial to ensure organizational learning by creating a culture that values reflection, feedback, and continuous improvement.

Lastly, encouraging innovation is essential for adaptive leaders, as it allows for creative problem-solving and the exploration of new possibilities.

By fostering an environment that promotes learning, innovation, and the ability to tackle complex challenges, you can unleash the true power of adaptive leadership.

Dealing with Complex Challenges

Navigating through intricate obstacles requires you to tap into your creative thinking abilities and foster innovative solutions. In today's complex world, leaders are faced with challenges that can't be solved through traditional means.

These challenges are often multi-faceted, involving various stakeholders and requiring a deep understanding of the underlying issues. To effectively deal with these challenges, leaders must embrace complexity and ambiguity and be willing to explore new ideas and perspectives.

They must encourage their teams to think outside the box and create an environment that fosters innovation and experimentation. By doing so, leaders can uncover new solutions, break through barriers, and ultimately drive meaningful change.

So, the next time you encounter a complex challenge, remember to tap into your creative thinking abilities, foster innovative solutions, and embrace the power of complexity.

Ensuring Organizational Learning

To ensure your organization's learning, you must foster a culture of curiosity and experimentation, allowing for mistakes and encouraging continuous improvement.

Embracing a mindset that values learning from failures and celebrates innovation will create an environment where employees feel empowered to explore new ideas and take risks.

Encourage open communication and collaboration among team members, providing opportunities for them to share their knowledge and experiences.

Implement feedback mechanisms and regular reflection processes to capture lessons learned and identify areas for improvement.

Utilize technology and data analytics to gather insights and drive evidence-based decision-making.

By actively promoting a learning culture, you can unlock the true potential of your organization and stay ahead in an ever-evolving business landscape.

Encouraging Innovation

Embracing a culture of curiosity and experimentation fosters innovation and creates an environment where you feel empowered to explore new ideas and take risks.

Encouraging innovation is crucial for organizations to stay competitive and adapt to a rapidly changing market.

By promoting a mindset that values creativity and rewards out-of-the-box thinking, you can inspire your team to come up with innovative solutions to challenges.

It's important to create channels for open communication and collaboration, providing opportunities for employees to share ideas and receive feedback.

Encouraging experimentation means allowing for failure as a learning opportunity and celebrating successes.

By supporting and nurturing innovation within your organization, you can unlock the true potential of your team and drive meaningful growth and success.

Chapter 16: Leadership and Decision Making

In Chapter 16, you'll dive into the topic of Leadership and Decision Making.

This chapter will help you understand the intricacies of decision-making in leadership roles and provide you with practical tips to improve your decision-making skills.

Furthermore, you'll learn how to effectively lead through difficult decisions, guiding your team through the challenges and uncertainties that arise.

Understanding Decision-Making in Leadership

When it comes to decision-making in leadership, there are several key points to consider.

First, understanding different decision-making models can help you make more informed choices and better assess the potential outcomes.

Second, it's important to recognize the impacts that your decisions can have, not only on your organization but also on your team and stakeholders.

Finally, ethical considerations should always be at the forefront of your decision-making process, ensuring that your choices align with your values and uphold the highest standards of integrity.

By taking these factors into account, you can unleash the true power of leadership and make decisions that drive positive change.

Decision Making Models

Let's explore decision-making models and discover their true power in leadership. Decision-making models are tools that leaders can use to make informed and effective decisions. These models provide a structured process for gathering information, analyzing options, and ultimately making a choice.

One commonly used model is the rational decision-making model, which involves identifying the problem, generating potential solutions, evaluating each option, and selecting the best one.

Another model is the intuitive decision-making model, which relies on gut feelings and instinct. This model is often used in situations where time is limited and there isn't enough information to make a rational decision.

Additionally, leaders can also use the participatory decision-making model, which involves involving team members in the decision-making process. This model not only fosters collaboration and engagement, but it also allows for diverse perspectives and ideas to be considered.

By understanding and utilizing decision-making models, leaders can make more informed and effective decisions, leading to better outcomes for their teams and organizations.

Impacts of Decisions

Interestingly enough, decision-making models have the potential to significantly influence the outcomes and consequences of the choices you make. By using a decision-making model, you can ensure that you consider all relevant factors and perspectives, leading to more informed and thoughtful decisions.

The impact of your decisions can be far-reaching, affecting not only your immediate team or organization, but also the larger ecosystem in which you operate. The decisions you make can shape the culture, values, and direction of your team, and can also have ripple effects on other departments and stakeholders.

Therefore, it's crucial to understand and evaluate the potential impacts of your decisions before making them. By doing so, you can maximize positive outcomes and minimize negative consequences, ultimately unleashing the true power of your leadership.

Ethical Considerations

Ethical considerations play a crucial role in decision-making, as they guide our choices towards what's morally right and just.

When faced with difficult decisions, it's important to consider not only the short-term gains or benefits but also the long-term consequences and impact on others.

Ethical considerations help us to take into account the perspectives and needs of different stakeholders, ensuring fairness and minimizing harm.

By making ethical considerations a priority, leaders can build trust and credibility, fostering a positive work environment and cultivating strong relationships with their team members.

Additionally, ethical decision-making promotes transparency and accountability, setting a standard for ethical behavior within an organization.

Ultimately, leaders who prioritize ethical considerations are more likely to make decisions that benefit not only themselves but also their team, organization, and society as a whole.

Improving Decision-Making Skills

When it comes to improving your decision-making skills, there are a few key points to keep in mind.

First, honing your critical thinking abilities will allow you to analyze situations more effectively and make informed decisions.

Additionally, developing your emotional intelligence will help you to understand and manage your own emotions, as well as empathize with and communicate effectively with others.

Lastly, collaboration and consensus-building are crucial skills to cultivate, as they enable you to harness the collective wisdom and expertise of a group to arrive at the best possible decision.

By focusing on these areas, you can enhance your decision-making skills and become a more effective leader.

Critical Thinking

Without critical thinking, leaders are like blindfolded drivers hurtling down the highway at top speed. Critical thinking is an essential skill that allows leaders to analyze situations, evaluate information, and make informed decisions. It involves questioning assumptions, challenging conventional wisdom, and considering multiple perspectives.

By cultivating critical thinking skills, leaders can navigate complex challenges, identify potential risks and opportunities, and devise effective strategies. Critical thinking enables leaders to separate fact from fiction, sift through the noise, and make sound judgments based on evidence and logic. It also fosters creativity and innovation, as leaders are encouraged to think outside the box and explore unconventional solutions.

In today's fast-paced and ever-changing business landscape, critical thinking is a crucial tool for leaders to unleash their true power and drive their organizations towards success.

Emotional Intelligence

Developing your emotional intelligence is the key to understanding and connecting with others on a deeper level, allowing you to build strong relationships and inspire loyalty among your team.

Emotional intelligence involves being aware of your own emotions and those of others, and using that awareness to manage interpersonal interactions effectively. By developing this skill, you can become more empathetic, understanding the perspectives and feelings of your team members, and responding in a way that fosters trust and collaboration.

Emotional intelligence also helps you navigate conflicts and difficult situations with grace and empathy, finding solutions that benefit everyone involved. It allows you to communicate more effectively, both verbally and non-verbally, picking up on cues and adjusting your approach accordingly.

Ultimately, emotional intelligence enables you to lead with authenticity and compassion, creating a positive and supportive work environment that brings out the best in your team.

Collaboration and Consensus-building

Collaboration and consensus-building are essential for creating a harmonious and productive work environment, allowing team members to come together and make collective decisions that drive success.

By working collaboratively, individuals can share their unique perspectives and expertise, leading to innovative and well-rounded solutions. Consensus-building ensures that everyone's opinions are considered and respected, fostering a sense of ownership and commitment to the final decision.

This approach also promotes effective communication and builds trust among team members, as they actively listen to one another and strive to find common ground.

Collaboration and consensus-building not only enhance the quality of decision-making but also create a supportive and inclusive culture where everyone feels valued and empowered.

By embracing these practices, leaders can unleash the true potential of their teams and achieve remarkable results.

Leading Through Difficult Decisions

When leading through difficult decisions, it's crucial to focus on risk assessment, stakeholder communication, and evaluation and adjustments.

By conducting a thorough risk assessment, you can identify potential obstacles and develop strategies to mitigate them.

Effective stakeholder communication ensures that all parties involved are informed and feel heard, fostering a sense of trust and collaboration.

Regular evaluation and adjustments allow you to adapt your decision-making process based on feedback and changing circumstances, increasing the chances of success.

Risk Assessment

Facing the unknown is like standing on the edge of a cliff, where leaders must accurately assess risks to navigate towards success. Risk assessment is a crucial skill that enables leaders to make informed decisions, identify potential threats, and anticipate the impact of their actions.

By evaluating the probability and potential consequences of various scenarios, leaders can develop strategies to mitigate risks and maximize opportunities. This process involves gathering relevant data, analyzing trends, consulting with experts, and considering alternative options.

Effective risk assessment empowers leaders to strike a balance between taking calculated risks and ensuring the overall well-being of their organization. It allows them to proactively address challenges, adapt to changing circumstances, and seize new opportunities.

Ultimately, by mastering the art of risk assessment, leaders can confidently steer their teams towards achieving their goals while minimizing potential setbacks.

Stakeholder Communication

To effectively communicate with stakeholders, you need to understand their needs, engage with them regularly, and keep them informed about the progress and challenges of your organization.

Stakeholders play a crucial role in the success of any organization, and their support and involvement are vital. By understanding their needs, you can tailor your communication to address their concerns and expectations.

Regular engagement with stakeholders allows you to build relationships, gain their trust, and foster a sense of partnership.

Keeping them informed about the progress and challenges of your organization ensures transparency and helps manage expectations.

Effective stakeholder communication enables you to align their interests with the goals of your organization, ultimately leading to better outcomes and success.

Evaluation and Adjustments

Take a moment to reflect on how you can make necessary adjustments and evaluate the progress you've made in order to achieve even greater success.

Evaluation and adjustments are crucial aspects of effective leadership. It allows you to assess the effectiveness of your strategies and tactics, identify areas for improvement, and make necessary changes to drive better results.

By regularly evaluating your progress, you can gain insights into what's working and what needs adjustment. This process enables you to adapt to changing circumstances, overcome obstacles, and stay on track towards your goals.

Consider gathering feedback from stakeholders, measuring key performance indicators, and analyzing data to inform your evaluation. Be open to constructive criticism and be willing to make the necessary adjustments to improve your leadership approach.

Remember, leadership isn't a static process, and continuous evaluation and adjustments are essential for unleashing your true power as a leader.

Chapter 17: Leadership and Innovation

In this chapter, you'll explore the crucial role that leadership plays in driving innovation within an organization. You'll learn about various innovation leadership styles and how they can be effectively applied to foster creativity and inspire a culture of innovation.

Additionally, the chapter will provide practical insights on building and nurturing an innovation team, highlighting the key strategies and practices that can enhance the effectiveness of such teams.

The Role of Leadership in Innovation

If you want to cultivate a culture of innovation within your organization, it's essential for you as a leader to unleash the true power of your leadership.

By encouraging your team to think outside the box and take risks, you can create an environment where innovative ideas can thrive.

Additionally, implementing these innovative ideas requires your active involvement and support, as you guide your team through the process and help turn ideas into reality.

And finally, in order to overcome resistance to change, you must lead by example and effectively communicate the benefits and opportunities that innovation can bring to your organization.

Cultivating a Culture of Innovation

Amidst the hustle and bustle of the modern workplace, fostering a culture of innovation is like sprinkling a dash of pixie dust that unleashes the true magic of leadership.

When leaders prioritize and cultivate a culture of innovation, they create an environment where creativity flourishes, new ideas are welcomed, and employees are empowered to think outside the box.

By encouraging risk-taking, embracing failure as a learning opportunity, and providing resources for experimentation, leaders can unleash the untapped potential within their teams.

A culture of innovation not only boosts productivity and drives business growth but also attracts and retains top talent who thrive in an environment that values and nurtures their creative instincts.

By creating an atmosphere that encourages collaboration, rewards innovative thinking, and fosters a growth mindset, leaders can unlock the true power of their teams and propel their organizations towards success in today's fast-paced and ever-evolving world.

Implementing Innovative Ideas

Creating an atmosphere that embraces and supports innovative ideas is essential for organizations to thrive in today's dynamic and rapidly changing business landscape.

As a leader, you have the power to shape the culture of your organization and encourage the implementation of innovative ideas. Start by fostering an environment that values creativity and encourages risk-taking.

Encourage your team members to think outside the box and explore new solutions to existing problems. Provide them with the necessary resources and support to turn their innovative ideas into reality.

Celebrate successes and learn from failures, creating a culture that views mistakes as opportunities for growth. By implementing innovative ideas, you can stay ahead of the competition, drive growth, and foster a culture of continuous improvement within your organization.

Overcoming Resistance to Change

To overcome resistance to change, you must engage your team and show them the benefits of embracing new ideas and ways of doing things. Start by creating an open and inclusive environment where everyone feels heard and valued. Encourage your team members to voice their concerns and fears about the proposed changes, and address those concerns with empathy and understanding.

Provide them with clear explanations of why the change is necessary and how it will benefit both the team and the organization as a whole. Offer concrete examples and success stories of other teams or organizations that have successfully implemented similar changes.

Additionally, involve your team in the decision-making process as much as possible, allowing them to have a sense of ownership and control over the changes. Provide training and resources to support them in adapting to the new ways of doing things.

Finally, celebrate and recognize the small wins along the way to keep morale high and motivate your team to continue embracing the change. By engaging your team and demonstrating the positive outcomes of change, you can overcome resistance and create a culture that embraces innovation and growth.

Innovation Leadership Styles

When it comes to innovation leadership styles, there are three key points to consider.

First, there is democratic innovation leadership, which involves empowering team members to contribute their ideas and make decisions collectively.

Second, there is transformational innovation leadership, which focuses on inspiring and motivating team members to think outside the box and embrace change.

Lastly, there is autocratic innovation leadership, where leaders take charge and make decisions on their own, without much input from others.

Understanding these different styles can help you navigate the challenges and opportunities of leading innovation effectively.

Democratic Innovation Leadership

Imagine a world where your innovative ideas as a leader aren't only welcomed, but actively encouraged and embraced by your team, leading to a truly democratic and powerful approach to leadership.

In democratic innovation leadership, the focus is on creating an environment where everyone's voice is valued and respected. This style of leadership empowers team members to contribute their unique perspectives and ideas, resulting in a more diverse and creative problem-solving process.

By involving team members in decision-making and giving them a sense of ownership, democratic leaders foster a culture of collaboration and trust. This approach doesn't only increase employee engagement and satisfaction, but also enhances the overall performance and productivity of the team.

As a democratic innovation leader, you have the opportunity to tap into the collective intelligence and unleash the true potential of your team, driving innovation and success.

Transformational Innovation Leadership

Step into the role of a transformational innovation leader and watch your team thrive as you inspire and empower them to reach new heights of creativity and success. As a transformational innovation leader, your main goal is to create a culture of continuous improvement and encourage your team to think outside the box.

You should actively seek out new ideas and encourage your team to do the same. By fostering an environment where innovative thinking is valued and rewarded, you can unleash the true potential of your team and drive them towards breakthrough solutions.

It is important to provide your team with the support and resources they need to experiment and take risks. Embrace failure as a learning opportunity and encourage your team to do the same. By fostering a sense of trust and psychological safety, you can create an environment where your team feels comfortable taking risks and pushing boundaries.

Finally, as a transformational innovation leader, it is crucial to lead by example. Show your team that you're willing to take risks, embrace new ideas, and continuously learn and grow. By embodying the qualities you want to see in your team, you can inspire and motivate them to do the same.

So step into the role of a transformational innovation leader and unlock the true power of leadership.

Autocratic Innovation Leadership

Embrace the absolute power and control as an autocratic innovation leader, and watch your team crumble under the weight of your micromanagement and lack of trust in their abilities.

By taking on the role of an autocratic leader in the realm of innovation, you may initially feel a sense of control and dominance. However, this approach stifles creativity and limits the potential for true innovation.

Your team members are capable individuals with unique perspectives and ideas, and by not allowing them the freedom to explore and take risks, you are hindering the very essence of innovation.

Instead, consider adopting a more collaborative and inclusive approach to leadership, where you empower your team to think outside the box, experiment, and learn from failures.

This way, you can truly unleash the power of innovation within your organization and achieve remarkable results.

Building an Innovation Team

When building an innovation team, it's crucial to select the right people who possess the necessary skills, knowledge, and mindset for creative problem-solving.

Encouraging creative thinking within the team is essential for generating innovative ideas and solutions.

Nurturing novel ideas involves creating a supportive environment where team members feel empowered to share and develop their unique perspectives.

This environment ultimately leads to breakthrough innovations.

Selecting the Right People

Surrounded by a skilled and passionate team, you feel a surge of confidence and envision the limitless potential you can unlock together.

Selecting the right people for your innovation team is crucial for success. Look for individuals who not only possess the necessary technical skills but also demonstrate a deep passion for their work. Seek out those who are open-minded, adaptable, and willing to challenge the status quo.

Diversity in backgrounds and experiences is also essential as it brings different perspectives and fresh ideas to the table. Additionally, consider their ability to collaborate and communicate effectively, as these skills are vital for a cohesive and productive team.

Remember, the right people will not only contribute their expertise but also inspire and motivate others to push boundaries and think outside the box.

Encouraging Creative Thinking

Fostering an environment that nurtures creative thinking allows ideas to flow freely, sparking innovation and opening new possibilities for growth.

When you encourage your team members to think outside the box and explore new solutions, you create a space where diverse perspectives and unique ideas can thrive.

By providing the necessary resources, support, and freedom to experiment, you empower individuals to unleash their true creative potential. This not only leads to breakthrough innovations but also strengthens the overall problem-solving capabilities of the team.

Creative thinking enables individuals to see beyond the obvious and challenge the status quo, paving the way for continuous improvement and adaptation in a rapidly changing world.

By embracing creative thinking, leaders can create a culture of innovation and drive their organizations towards success.

Nurturing Novel Ideas

Nurturing novel ideas allows for the cultivation of innovative thinking and the exploration of uncharted territories in problem-solving. By creating an environment that encourages and values new and unconventional ideas, leaders can unlock the true potential of their teams.

When individuals feel safe to share their unique perspectives, they're more likely to think outside the box and come up with groundbreaking solutions. To foster the growth of novel ideas, leaders can implement practices such as brainstorming sessions, idea-sharing platforms, and cross-functional collaborations. These initiatives not only promote creativity but also foster a sense of ownership and engagement among team members.

Furthermore, leaders should actively listen to and validate these novel ideas, providing constructive feedback and support to help refine and develop them. By nurturing novel ideas, leaders can empower their teams to push boundaries, challenge the status quo, and ultimately drive innovation and growth.

Chapter 18: Servant Leadership

In this chapter on Servant Leadership, you'll explore the definition and characteristics of this leadership style.

You'll learn how Servant Leadership can be manifested in various organizational settings, and gain practical tips on how to practice this leadership approach.

By understanding the essence of Servant Leadership, you'll be able to unleash its true power and make a positive impact as a leader.

Defining Servant Leadership

In this discussion, you'll explore the principles of Servant Leadership and discover how it goes beyond authority to unleash the true power of leadership.

You'll also uncover the benefits of adopting a servant leadership approach, such as increased employee satisfaction and improved team performance.

Finally, you'll delve into the criticism surrounding servant leadership, understanding both its limitations and potential drawbacks.

Get ready to gain valuable insights into this transformative leadership style.

Principles of Servant Leadership

Discover the transformative power of servant leadership and how it can empower you to lead with compassion and humility.

Servant leadership is founded on several key principles that guide leaders in their approach to leading others.

First and foremost, it emphasizes the importance of putting the needs of others before your own. By prioritizing the well-being and growth of your team members, you create an environment that fosters trust and collaboration.

Additionally, servant leadership encourages active listening and empathy, recognizing that understanding the perspectives and emotions of those you lead is crucial for effective leadership.

It also promotes empowerment, giving individuals the autonomy and support they need to succeed.

Lastly, servant leadership embraces a long-term perspective, focusing on the development and growth of individuals and the organization as a whole.

By embodying these principles, you can unleash the true power of leadership and create a positive and impactful work environment.

Benefits of Servant Leadership

Now that you have a deeper understanding of the principles of Servant Leadership, let's explore the benefits that this approach can bring to both leaders and their teams.

By embracing Servant Leadership, you can create a work environment where trust, collaboration, and empathy thrive. As a leader, you'll empower your team members to reach their full potential by putting their needs and growth first. This selfless approach not only fosters a sense of belonging and loyalty among your team, but it also enhances their motivation and engagement.

By actively listening to their ideas and concerns, you can make better-informed decisions that align with their needs and aspirations. Furthermore, Servant Leadership promotes a culture of continuous learning and development, which ultimately leads to higher productivity and performance.

So, by embracing this leadership style, you can unleash the true power of your team and achieve remarkable results.

Criticism of Servant Leadership

One interesting statistic to consider is that while servant leadership is highly regarded for its positive impact on employee engagement and satisfaction, a study found that only 28% of leaders actually practice this approach consistently.

This criticism stems from the perception that servant leadership might be too idealistic or soft, and some leaders may feel that they need to maintain a more authoritative or directive style in order to get results. Additionally, implementing servant leadership requires a significant shift in mindset and behavior, which can be challenging for leaders who are used to more traditional hierarchical approaches.

However, it's important to recognize that servant leadership is not about being a pushover or relinquishing control, but rather about empowering and serving others to achieve collective success. By embracing this approach, leaders can foster a culture of trust, collaboration, and innovation, ultimately leading to higher employee morale and organizational performance.

Manifesting Servant Leadership

When it comes to manifesting servant leadership, there are three key points to focus on:

1. Listening: By actively listening to your team members, you show them that their voices matter and that you value their input.

2. Empathy: Cultivating empathy allows you to understand and relate to others on a deeper level, fostering a sense of trust and connection.

3. Stewardship: Lastly, practicing stewardship means taking responsibility for the well-being of both your team and the organization as a whole, making decisions that prioritize their long-term success.

By embodying these qualities, you can truly unleash the power of servant leadership and create a positive and effective work environment.

Listening

As you listen intently and empathetically to others, the true power of your leadership begins to unfold.

Listening isn't just about hearing the words that are being spoken, but it's about truly understanding and connecting with the person who's speaking.

It requires you to set aside your own agenda and fully engage in the conversation.

When you listen in this way, you create an environment where people feel valued and heard.

It allows you to gain a deeper understanding of the challenges and needs of your team, which in turn enables you to make more informed decisions and provide the necessary support.

By actively listening, you're able to build trust and rapport with your team, fostering a sense of collaboration and unity.

So, take the time to listen to your team members, to their ideas, concerns, and aspirations.

It's through listening that you can truly unleash the power of your leadership and create a positive and productive work environment.

Empathy

Immerse yourself in the experiences of others, truly connecting with their emotions and understanding their perspective, allowing empathy to weave a tapestry of understanding and compassion among your team.

Empathy is the key to effective leadership, as it allows you to see beyond the surface and truly understand the needs and concerns of your team members.

By putting yourself in their shoes, you can gain valuable insights into their motivations and challenges, and this understanding can help you to better support and guide them.

Empathy also fosters a sense of trust and belonging within your team, as it shows that you genuinely care about their well-being and are willing to listen and support them.

In a world where people often feel disconnected and unheard, being an empathetic leader can make a significant impact, not only in the workplace but also in the lives of your team members.

So, take the time to listen and understand, and let empathy guide your leadership approach.

Stewardship

Now that you've explored the importance of empathy in leadership, it's time to delve into another key aspect: stewardship.

As a leader, your role extends beyond just managing and directing others. Stewardship is about taking responsibility for the well-being and success of your team, the organization, and the larger community.

It involves being a caretaker, a guardian, and a champion for the people and resources under your care.

By adopting a mindset of stewardship, you can create a culture of trust, collaboration, and growth. It means making decisions that prioritize the long-term sustainability and impact of your actions, rather than just seeking short-term gains.

Stewardship requires a deep understanding of your team's needs and aspirations, and a commitment to their development and success. By embracing stewardship, you can unleash the true power of your leadership and create a lasting impact that goes beyond authority.

Practicing Servant Leadership

When practicing servant leadership, it's crucial to engage in self-reflection to understand your own strengths and weaknesses as a leader.

This allows you to continuously improve and better serve your team.

Balancing servitude and authority is another key aspect of servant leadership. It involves leading with humility while still providing guidance and direction.

Additionally, encouraging team development is essential. It empowers individuals to grow and thrive, ultimately benefiting the team as a whole.

Self-reflection

Explore the depths of your own thoughts and emotions, allowing yourself to truly understand the power of self-reflection.

Take a moment to pause and look inward, examining your actions, motivations, and beliefs.

Self-reflection is a vital tool for personal growth and leadership development. It enables you to gain clarity, uncover blind spots, and make conscious choices.

Through self-reflection, you can identify your strengths and weaknesses, understand your triggers and patterns, and cultivate self-awareness.

This process allows you to better understand yourself, your values, and your purpose, which in turn empowers you to lead with authenticity and integrity.

By regularly engaging in self-reflection, you can continuously learn and grow, making better decisions and building stronger relationships.

So, take the time to delve into your own thoughts and emotions, and embrace the transformative power of self-reflection in your leadership journey.

Balancing Servitude and Authority

Find the delicate equilibrium between serving others and exerting your influence, embodying the harmony of a conductor guiding an orchestra.

As a leader, it's crucial to strike a balance between being a servant and exercising authority.

On one hand, you must be willing to serve and support your team, understanding their needs and providing the necessary resources and guidance to help them succeed. This means being approachable, empathetic, and actively listening to their concerns and ideas.

On the other hand, you must also assert your authority and make tough decisions when necessary. This requires setting clear expectations, holding people accountable, and making difficult choices that may not always be popular.

By finding this delicate balance, you can create a work environment that encourages collaboration, empowers individuals, and ultimately drives success.

Remember, leadership isn't about wielding power over others, but rather about using your influence to bring out the best in everyone around you.

Encouraging Team Development

To truly excel as a leader, you must actively foster the growth and development of your team, encouraging them to reach their full potential.

One of the most effective ways to do this is by creating a culture of continuous learning and improvement within your team. Encourage your team members to take on new challenges and expand their skill sets. Provide them with opportunities for professional development, such as attending conferences or workshops, or even just assigning them new projects that push them out of their comfort zones. By investing in their growth, you not only enhance their individual abilities but also strengthen the overall capability of your team.

Additionally, be sure to provide regular feedback and recognition to your team members. Recognize their achievements and acknowledge their contributions. This will not only boost their morale but also motivate them to continue striving for excellence.

Furthermore, create an environment where collaboration and teamwork are valued. Encourage your team members to share their ideas, collaborate on projects, and support one another. By fostering a sense of camaraderie and collaboration, you create a team that is not only more productive but also more innovative and resilient.

Ultimately, by encouraging team development, you unleash the true power of your leadership and create a team that is capable of achieving extraordinary results.

Chapter 19: Leadership in Non-Profit Organizations

In this chapter, you'll explore the unique challenges that non-profit leaders face and the skills they need to navigate these challenges effectively.

You'll gain insights into the specific demands of leadership in non-profit organizations and discover strategies for success.

Additionally, you'll be inspired by real-life success stories of leaders in the non-profit sector, providing practical examples of effective leadership in action.

Unique Challenges for Non-Profit Leaders

As a non-profit leader, you face unique challenges that go beyond traditional authority. Limited resources can make it difficult to achieve your organization's goals, requiring you to be creative and strategic in your approach.

Engaging stakeholders is crucial for building support and partnerships, but it can also be challenging to navigate different perspectives and interests.

Finally, aligning your mission and vision with those of your team and stakeholders is essential for driving collective impact and ensuring long-term success.

Limited Resources

Despite the limited resources, the small startup was able to successfully launch a new product and gain market share.

In the world of non-profit leadership, limited resources are a common challenge that leaders face. With limited funding and manpower, it can be difficult to make a significant impact. However, successful non-profit leaders understand the importance of maximizing the resources they do have.

They prioritize their efforts and focus on initiatives that will yield the greatest results. They leverage partnerships and collaborations to stretch their limited resources even further. They also think creatively and find innovative solutions to tackle problems without breaking the bank.

By taking a strategic approach and making the most of their limited resources, non-profit leaders can overcome this challenge and achieve their goals.

Stakeholder Engagement

Now that you've learned about the challenges of limited resources, it's time to explore the importance of stakeholder engagement in unleashing the true power of leadership.

Engaging stakeholders is crucial for leaders to achieve their goals and drive positive change. By involving stakeholders, whether they're employees, customers, or community members, leaders can gather valuable insights, build trust, and foster collaboration.

Stakeholder engagement goes beyond simply communicating with others; it involves actively listening to their perspectives, understanding their concerns, and involving them in decision-making processes. Effective stakeholder engagement creates a sense of ownership and shared responsibility, leading to more innovative solutions and greater buy-in from all parties involved.

So, as a leader, make it a priority to engage your stakeholders and tap into their diverse knowledge and expertise to unlock the true potential of your leadership.

Mission and Vision Alignment

Aligning your mission and vision is like bringing together the pieces of a puzzle, creating a clear and inspiring picture of the future you aspire to achieve. By aligning your mission, which defines your purpose and the impact you want to make, with your vision, which outlines the desired future state, you create a powerful roadmap for success.

When your mission and vision are aligned, it becomes easier to make decisions, set goals, and prioritize actions that move you closer to your desired outcome. It also provides a sense of direction and purpose for your team, helping them understand the why behind their work and motivating them to contribute their best efforts.

When everyone is working towards a shared vision, collaboration and synergy are maximized, leading to improved performance and results. So take the time to align your mission and vision, and watch as your organization transforms into a focused and purpose-driven powerhouse.

Skills for Non-Profit Leaders

As a non-profit leader, it's crucial to possess the skills of fundraising, partnering, and collaboration, and strategic planning.

Fundraising is essential for securing the necessary resources to support your organization's mission and programs.

Partnering and collaboration allow you to leverage the strengths and expertise of other organizations and individuals, maximizing your impact and reach.

Strategic planning helps you set clear goals and objectives, prioritize initiatives, and ensure long-term sustainability for your non-profit.

By honing these skills, you can effectively lead your organization towards success and make a lasting difference in your community.

Fundraising

By boldly brainstorming unique fundraising strategies, you can captivate potential donors and create a cascade of contributions.

Think outside the box and consider innovative approaches that align with your organization's mission and values.

Engage your community by hosting events that not only raise funds but also raise awareness about your cause.

Collaborate with local businesses to create win-win partnerships, where they can contribute a portion of their profits to your organization.

Leverage the power of social media to reach a wider audience and make it easy for people to donate online.

Show your donors the impact of their contributions by sharing success stories and testimonials. Additionally, consider offering incentives or rewards to encourage larger donations.

Remember, fundraising isn't just about asking for money, it's about building relationships and inspiring others to join your cause. So, be creative, authentic, and passionate in your fundraising efforts, and watch as the contributions pour in to support your non-profit's mission.

Partnering and Collaboration

Forge partnerships and collaborate with other organizations to amplify your impact and create a stronger collective force for change. By partnering with like-minded organizations, you can pool your resources, expertise, and networks to achieve common goals more effectively.

Collaboration allows you to tap into different perspectives and ideas, fostering innovation and creativity. It also enables you to leverage each other's strengths and fill in any gaps in your own capabilities.

Through partnerships, you can access new funding opportunities, expand your reach, and increase your influence. Building strong relationships with other organizations can lead to long-term collaborations and a shared commitment to making a positive difference.

Remember, collaboration is not just about sharing resources, but also about building trust, fostering open communication, and embracing diversity. By working together, you can achieve greater impact and create meaningful change in your community and beyond.

Strategic Planning

Plan strategically and align your goals and actions to maximize your impact and drive positive change.

Strategic planning is a crucial aspect of leadership that allows you to set a clear direction for your organization and ensure that all efforts are focused on achieving the desired outcomes.

By taking the time to analyze your current situation, identify opportunities and potential obstacles, and develop a comprehensive plan, you can make informed decisions and prioritize your actions effectively.

This process involves setting specific, measurable, achievable, relevant, and time-bound goals that are aligned with your organization's mission and vision.

It also includes identifying the resources, capabilities, and partnerships needed to support your plan and monitoring progress along the way.

By engaging your team in the strategic planning process, you can foster a sense of ownership and commitment, resulting in increased motivation and collaboration.

Strategic planning enables you to anticipate and adapt to changes in the external environment, identify emerging trends and opportunities, and proactively respond to challenges.

It empowers you to make informed decisions, allocate resources efficiently, and navigate complex situations with clarity and purpose.

Ultimately, strategic planning allows you to unleash the true power of leadership by driving meaningful and sustainable change in your organization and beyond.

Leadership Success Stories in Non-Profit Sector

In the non-profit sector, leadership success stories are abundant, showcasing the accomplishments and impact that can be achieved through effective leadership. These leaders have achieved remarkable accomplishments. They have successfully raised significant funds for their organizations, mobilized communities, and driven positive change. Along the way, they have learned valuable lessons about the importance of building strong relationships, communicating effectively, and adapting to ever-changing circumstances.

Accomplishments

Amidst the chaos, you're able to wield your accomplishments like shining beacons, guiding your team towards success.

Your accomplishments serve as proof of your leadership capabilities and inspire confidence in your team.

When you achieve your goals and exceed expectations, you demonstrate your ability to overcome challenges and make a positive impact.

These accomplishments also provide a sense of direction and purpose for your team, showing them what's possible and motivating them to strive for greatness.

By celebrating your accomplishments, you create a culture of success and inspire your team to continue pushing boundaries and achieving new heights.

So, embrace your accomplishments and let them serve as a powerful tool to unleash the true power of your leadership.

Lessons Learned

During times of chaos, you can gain valuable insights from the lessons learned, helping you grow as a leader and improve team performance.

Did you know that 70% of leaders believe that learning from past mistakes is essential for success?

Reflecting on your past experiences allows you to identify areas for improvement and make necessary adjustments to your leadership style.

By analyzing what went wrong and understanding the underlying causes, you can develop strategies to prevent similar issues in the future.

Additionally, learning from mistakes fosters a culture of continuous improvement within your team.

Encouraging open and honest communication about lessons learned creates a safe space for team members to share their experiences and insights.

This collaborative approach enables everyone to learn from each other's mistakes, ultimately enhancing overall team performance.

Remember, as a leader, your ability to acknowledge and learn from failures is a powerful tool in your journey towards effective leadership.

Chapter 20: Charismatic Leadership

In Chapter 20, you'll explore the concept of charismatic leadership and its significance in the realm of non-profit organizations.

Understanding charisma in leadership is crucial as it allows you to tap into the true power of your influence.

You'll also learn practical strategies for building charisma as a leader, enabling you to inspire and motivate others towards a common goal.

Understanding Charisma in Leadership

Do you want to understand the true power of leadership beyond authority? Then it's important to explore the concept of charisma.

Charisma, defined as the ability to inspire and influence others, plays a significant role in leadership. It has a profound impact on followers, motivating them to perform at their best.

However, it's crucial for leaders to balance charisma with humility, as excessive charisma can sometimes overshadow the contributions and potential of others.

Definition of Charisma

Imagine yourself in the presence of a charismatic leader, feeling the undeniable magnetic pull of their captivating presence and inspiring energy.

Charisma, in the realm of leadership, is a quality that sets certain individuals apart from the rest. It is a compelling and attractive force that draws people towards them, and makes them stand out in a crowd.

Charismatic leaders possess a unique ability to inspire and motivate others, effortlessly commanding attention and respect. They have a natural charm and confidence that captivates those around them, making people want to follow their lead.

This quality is not something that can be taught or learned, but rather it is an innate characteristic that some individuals possess. Charisma is not just about being charming or likeable, but it involves a deep sense of authenticity and genuine connection with others.

It is about having a clear vision, strong values, and the ability to communicate effectively, all while exuding a sense of enthusiasm and passion.

Charismatic leaders have the power to influence and inspire others to achieve greatness, making them truly remarkable and influential figures in the realm of leadership.

Impact of Charisma on Followers

Now that you understand the definition of charisma, it's important to explore the impact it has on followers.

Charismatic leaders have a unique ability to inspire and motivate their followers to achieve great things. They possess a magnetic presence that draws people towards them and makes them want to follow their lead.

When a leader exudes charisma, it creates a sense of excitement and enthusiasm among their followers. People are willing to go above and beyond their regular duties because they believe in the vision and message of the charismatic leader.

Charisma has the power to ignite passion, build trust, and foster a strong sense of loyalty among followers. It creates a positive and energizing environment where everyone feels motivated to work towards a common goal.

The impact of charisma on followers cannot be underestimated, as it has the potential to transform ordinary individuals into extraordinary achievers.

Balancing Charisma and Humility

Find the delicate equilibrium between your magnetic charisma and humble demeanor, as it's the key to building genuine connections with your followers.

While charisma can be a powerful tool in influencing others, it must be tempered with humility to avoid alienating those around you.

By acknowledging and valuing the contributions and perspectives of others, you demonstrate a willingness to listen and learn, fostering an environment of trust and respect.

Balancing charisma with humility also allows you to connect on a deeper level with your followers, as they see you as approachable and relatable.

This combination of traits enables you to inspire and motivate others while remaining grounded and genuine.

Remember, true leadership isn't about dominating others with your charisma, but about empowering and uplifting them through your humility.

Building Charisma as a Leader

To build charisma as a leader, it's essential to exude confidence and optimism. By demonstrating a positive attitude and belief in yourself and your team, you inspire others to follow your lead.

Additionally, articulating a clear vision is crucial in gaining the trust and support of your team. When you can clearly communicate your goals and objectives, it helps to align everyone's efforts towards a common purpose.

Lastly, building strong relationships is key to developing charisma as a leader. By fostering connections and showing genuine interest in others, you create a sense of camaraderie and loyalty within your team.

Confidence and Optimism

Unleash the true power of leadership by embracing confidence and optimism.

As a leader, it's crucial to exude confidence in your abilities and in the vision you have for your team.

When you believe in yourself and your capabilities, it inspires trust and motivates others to follow your lead.

Confidence allows you to make decisions with conviction and take calculated risks, which are essential for driving your team towards success.

Additionally, optimism plays a vital role in leadership.

By maintaining a positive outlook, you create an environment that fosters innovation, resilience, and a can-do attitude.

Your optimism becomes contagious, and it empowers your team to overcome challenges and stay focused on achieving goals.

So, embrace confidence and optimism as a leader, and watch as you unlock the true power within yourself and those around you.

Articulating a Clear Vision

Embrace the power of articulating a clear vision and watch as your team comes together, inspired and driven to achieve their shared goals.

When you're able to clearly communicate your vision, you provide your team with a sense of direction and purpose. By painting a vivid picture of the future you envision, you create a roadmap for success and ignite a sense of passion within your team members.

A clear vision helps your team understand the why behind their work, allowing them to see the bigger picture and the impact they can make. It also fosters unity and collaboration, as everyone aligns their efforts towards a common goal.

When your team shares a clear vision, it becomes easier to make decisions, prioritize tasks, and stay focused on what truly matters.

So take the time to articulate your vision with clarity and conviction, and witness the transformational power it has in unleashing the true potential of your team.

Building Strong Relationships

Building strong relationships is essential for effective leadership as it cultivates trust and fosters collaboration among team members.

When you invest time and effort in building relationships with your team, you create a supportive environment where individuals feel valued and understood.

By actively listening, empathizing, and showing genuine interest in their ideas and concerns, you establish a foundation of trust that encourages open communication and transparency.

Strong relationships also foster collaboration, as team members are more likely to share their knowledge, skills, and perspectives when they feel connected and respected. This collaboration leads to innovative solutions and increased productivity.

Additionally, building strong relationships outside of your team, such as with stakeholders and other leaders, can enhance your influence and effectiveness as a leader.

By nurturing these relationships, you can develop partnerships, gain support, and leverage resources to drive positive change.

In conclusion, building strong relationships is not only a fundamental aspect of effective leadership but also a practical strategy that can bring about meaningful results for both individuals and organizations.

Chapter 21: Leadership Challenges in the 21st Century

In Chapter 21, you'll delve into the various challenges that leaders face in the modern world.

You'll explore the essential skills that leaders need to possess in the 21st century, such as adaptability, digital literacy, and global mindset.

Additionally, you'll learn strategies on how to overcome these modern challenges and lead your team to success.

Modern Leadership Challenges

In today's rapidly changing world, leaders face numerous challenges that go beyond traditional authority. Rapid technological change has revolutionized the way we work and communicate, requiring leaders to adapt and embrace new tools and strategies.

Globalization has increased the complexity of business operations, forcing leaders to navigate cultural differences and collaborate with diverse teams. Additionally, evolving roles and expectations mean that leaders must be flexible, agile, and capable of inspiring and empowering others.

Embracing these challenges and unleashing the true power of leadership can help organizations thrive in the modern era.

Rapid Technological Change

Embrace the rapid technological change and let it fuel your innovative spirit, unlocking your true potential as a leader.

In today's fast-paced world, technology is evolving at an unprecedented rate, presenting both challenges and opportunities for leaders. To stay ahead, it's crucial to embrace these changes and leverage them to drive innovation in your organization.

Rapid technological advancements can enable you to streamline processes, enhance productivity, and improve customer experiences. By understanding the latest technologies and their potential applications, you can make informed decisions that'll propel your business forward.

Additionally, technology can foster collaboration and communication, allowing you to connect with your team and stakeholders on a global scale.

Embracing rapid technological change also requires a mindset shift, as it requires leaders to be open to new ideas, adaptable, and continuously learning. By embracing and harnessing technology, you can unleash your true power as a leader and navigate the ever-changing landscape of the digital age.

Globalization

Take a leap and explore the vast opportunities that globalization offers, allowing you to spread your wings and connect with a diverse range of individuals and markets.

In today's interconnected world, globalization has become the driving force behind economic growth and innovation. It has opened up new avenues for businesses to expand their reach and tap into untapped markets.

With globalization, you have the chance to collaborate with people from different cultures, exchange ideas, and gain a fresh perspective on solving problems. Moreover, it enables you to access a global talent pool, bringing together the best minds from around the world to work towards a common goal.

By embracing globalization, you can leverage these diverse perspectives and talents, leading to increased creativity, productivity, and competitiveness.

So, don't shy away from this global landscape; instead, seize the opportunity to connect, learn, and thrive in the ever-evolving global marketplace.

Evolving Roles and Expectations

Step into the ever-evolving global landscape and discover the changing roles and expectations that await you, as you navigate through a world of endless possibilities and dynamic challenges.

In this rapidly changing world, leadership is no longer confined to traditional hierarchies and authority. It has become a fluid and adaptable concept that requires individuals to be agile, innovative, and collaborative.

Today's leaders are expected to be visionaries, able to anticipate and embrace change, and guide their organizations towards success in an uncertain future. They must possess a global mindset, understanding the interconnectedness of different cultures and economies, and leverage diversity as a source of strength.

Moreover, leaders are now expected to be ethical and socially responsible, taking into account the impact of their decisions on the environment, society, and future generations. They must lead by example, inspiring their teams to adopt sustainable practices and contribute to the greater good.

This evolving landscape demands leaders who are not afraid to challenge the status quo, who can think outside the box and embrace innovation. They must be lifelong learners, constantly seeking new knowledge and skills to stay ahead in a rapidly changing world.

By embracing these evolving roles and expectations, you can unleash the true power of leadership and make a lasting impact in an ever-changing global landscape.

21st Century Skills for Leaders

In the 21st century, leaders need to possess a set of skills that go beyond traditional leadership qualities.

Three key skills that are crucial for leaders in today's digital age are digital literacy, cross-cultural competence, and emotional intelligence.

Digital literacy is essential for leaders to navigate and leverage the constantly evolving digital landscape, while cross-cultural competence enables leaders to effectively collaborate with individuals from diverse backgrounds.

Additionally, emotional intelligence allows leaders to understand and manage their own emotions, as well as empathize and connect with others, fostering a positive and inclusive work environment.

Digital Literacy

With the world becoming increasingly digitized, leaders who possess strong digital literacy skills are more likely to navigate the complexities of the digital age and stay ahead of the curve, as the adage goes, 'knowledge is power.'

In today's fast-paced and technology-driven world, it's crucial for leaders to understand and harness the power of digital tools and platforms.

Digital literacy encompasses the ability to effectively use and leverage technology, including social media, data analytics, and online collaboration tools, to achieve organizational goals and drive innovation.

Leaders who are digitally literate can make informed decisions based on data and insights, connect with a global network of professionals, and adapt quickly to changing market trends.

Furthermore, digital literacy enables leaders to communicate and engage with their teams and stakeholders in a more efficient and impactful manner.

By embracing digital literacy, leaders can unlock new opportunities, streamline processes, and create a culture of innovation within their organizations.

So, whether it's mastering the art of data analysis or staying up to date with the latest digital trends, developing strong digital literacy skills is essential for leaders who want to thrive in today's digital world.

Cross-Cultural Competence

Now that you've developed your digital literacy skills, it's time to explore another essential aspect of effective leadership: cross-cultural competence. In today's globalized world, being able to navigate and work with people from different cultures is crucial for success.

Cross-cultural competence goes beyond simply tolerating cultural differences; it involves understanding, appreciating, and adapting to diverse perspectives, beliefs, and customs. By honing your cross-cultural competence, you can foster stronger relationships, build trust, and create inclusive environments where everyone feels valued and understood.

This skill will not only enhance your leadership abilities but also enable you to navigate the complexities of an interconnected world with confidence and grace. So, let's embark on this journey of cultural exploration and equip ourselves with the tools needed to bridge gaps and connect with people from all walks of life.

Emotional Intelligence

Emotional intelligence is a key skill for successful and impactful leadership. As a leader, it's crucial to understand and manage your own emotions, as well as the emotions of those around you. By being aware of your own emotions and how they impact your decision-making and interactions with others, you can better navigate challenging situations and make more effective choices.

Additionally, by being empathetic and understanding the emotions of your team members, you can build stronger relationships, inspire trust, and create a positive and supportive work environment. Developing emotional intelligence involves actively listening to others, recognizing and managing your own emotions, and practicing empathy and understanding.

By honing this skill, you can become a more effective leader and drive meaningful change within your organization.

Overcoming Modern Challenges

In order to overcome modern challenges as a leader, it's essential that you embrace continuous learning.

This means staying up-to-date with the latest industry trends, technologies, and best practices.

Additionally, you must be willing to embrace change and adapt to new situations and circumstances.

Lastly, encouraging diversity within your team and organization is crucial as it brings in different perspectives and ideas, leading to innovation and better decision-making.

Continuous Learning

Learning is a never-ending journey that allows you, as a leader, to tap into your full potential. Continuous learning is essential in today's fast-paced and ever-evolving world. It enables you to stay ahead of the curve, adapt to new challenges, and make informed decisions.

By continuously learning, you can expand your knowledge, skills, and perspectives, which ultimately enhances your leadership capabilities. Whether it's attending workshops, reading books, or seeking feedback from your team, embracing a mindset of continuous learning will enable you to grow personally and professionally. It also demonstrates to your team and organization that you're dedicated to self-improvement and open to new ideas.

So, make it a priority to invest in your own development and commit to a lifelong learning journey. The benefits aren't only for you but also for those you lead, as you'll be better equipped to navigate the complexities of leadership, inspire others, and drive meaningful change.

Embracing Change

By embracing change, you can unlock your full potential as a leader and create a powerful ripple effect that inspires and motivates your team members to embrace growth and innovation.

Change is inevitable in today's fast-paced and ever-evolving world, and as a leader, it's crucial to not only adapt to change but also embrace it. Embracing change allows you to stay ahead of the curve, seize new opportunities, and navigate through challenges with agility and resilience. It requires a mindset shift from viewing change as a threat to seeing it as an opportunity for growth and improvement.

By fostering a culture of embracing change within your team, you encourage continuous learning and innovation. You empower your team members to think outside the box, explore new ideas, and take calculated risks. Change becomes a catalyst for creativity and collaboration, propelling your team towards achieving their goals and driving organizational success.

As a leader, it's important to lead by example and demonstrate your openness to change. Show your team that change isn't something to fear but rather a chance to evolve and thrive. Embracing change also involves effective communication, as you need to clearly articulate the reasons behind the change and the vision for the future.

By involving your team in the change process and providing support and resources, you create a sense of ownership and commitment, ensuring a smoother transition.

So, embrace change and unleash the true power of your leadership to inspire, motivate, and drive your team towards excellence and innovation.

Encouraging Diversity

Get ready to shake things up and make your team truly diverse - it's time to embrace the beauty of differences and create a melting pot of ideas and perspectives!

Encouraging diversity in your team is not just about ticking boxes or meeting quotas; it's about harnessing the power of different backgrounds, experiences, and perspectives to drive innovation and creativity. By valuing diversity, you open up new avenues for problem-solving and decision-making, leading to better outcomes for your organization.

Embracing diversity also fosters a culture of inclusion and belonging, where every team member feels valued and respected. To encourage diversity, start by creating an inclusive environment where everyone feels comfortable expressing their unique viewpoints. Actively seek out and recruit individuals from different backgrounds, ensuring that your team represents a wide range of perspectives.

Encourage open and respectful communication, where ideas are debated and discussed without fear of judgment. Emphasize the importance of diversity in team meetings and discussions, highlighting the benefits it brings to the table. Finally, lead by example and demonstrate your commitment to diversity in your actions and decision-making.

By embracing diversity, you will unlock the true power of leadership and create a team that thrives on the richness of its differences.

Chapter 22: The Relationship Between Power and Leadership

In Chapter 22, you'll delve into the relationship between power and leadership.

You'll gain a deeper understanding of power in leadership and how it can be effectively utilized.

Additionally, you'll explore the importance of balancing power and influence in leadership, learning practical strategies to maintain a harmonious equilibrium.

Understanding Power in Leadership

When it comes to leadership, understanding power is crucial. You need to recognize the role that power plays in your leadership style and how it can influence others.

There are different types of power, such as legitimate power, expert power, and referent power, each with its own strengths and weaknesses.

Finally, be aware of the potential pitfalls of power, such as becoming too authoritarian or abusing your power, as these can have detrimental effects on your team and overall success.

The Role of Power

Imagine the incredible impact you can have when you fully embrace and wield the true power of leadership.

The role of power in leadership is not about controlling or dominating others, but rather about inspiring and empowering them to reach their full potential.

As a leader, your power lies in your ability to listen, understand, and connect with your team members. By building trust and fostering a collaborative environment, you can create a sense of shared purpose and motivate others to give their best.

Your power also comes from your vision and the ability to communicate it effectively. By articulating a compelling vision and setting clear goals, you can inspire and guide your team towards success.

Additionally, your power as a leader is manifested in your decision-making ability. By making informed and inclusive decisions, you can create a sense of trust and accountability within your team.

Ultimately, the role of power in leadership is not about exerting control, but about creating an environment where everyone feels valued, empowered, and motivated to contribute their best.

Types of Power

With the different types of power found in leadership, you can unleash a force that propels your team towards success like a gust of wind guiding a sailboat. Understanding the various types of power is essential for leaders who want to effectively influence and motivate their team.

One type of power is legitimate power, which is derived from your formal position or authority within the organization. This power gives you the ability to make decisions and enforce them.

Another type of power is expert power, which comes from your knowledge, skills, and expertise in a particular area. When you possess expert power, your team looks to you for guidance and trusts your judgment.

Additionally, referent power is another type of power that stems from your personal qualities and charisma. It is the power that comes from being respected and admired by others. When you have referent power, your team is more likely to follow your lead and be influenced by your actions.

Lastly, there is coercive power, which is based on punishments and threats. While coercive power can sometimes be effective in getting short-term compliance, it is not a sustainable or long-term solution.

By understanding and harnessing the different types of power, you can create a leadership style that inspires and motivates your team to reach their full potential.

Potential Pitfalls of Power

Beware of the potential traps that come with having too much control and influence. While power can be a great asset in leadership, it also carries certain pitfalls that we need to be aware of.

One of the biggest dangers is becoming detached from reality and losing touch with the needs and concerns of those you lead. When you have too much power, it's easy to fall into a mindset of arrogance and entitlement, which can lead to a lack of empathy and understanding.

Another pitfall is the temptation to abuse power for personal gain or to manipulate others. This can erode trust and damage relationships, ultimately undermining your effectiveness as a leader.

Additionally, having too much power can create a culture of fear and intimidation, stifling creativity and innovation. It's important to remember that true leadership is not about control, but about inspiring and empowering others.

So, as you navigate the realm of power, be mindful of these potential pitfalls and strive to use your influence in a way that benefits everyone involved.

Balancing Power and Influence in Leadership

In this discussion, you'll explore the importance of balancing power and influence in leadership through three key points.

Firstly, you'll delve into the ethical use of power, understanding how to wield it responsibly and with integrity.

Secondly, you'll learn about empowering others, discovering strategies to support and uplift your team members, enabling them to reach their full potential.

Lastly, you'll examine the shift from power over to power with, understanding the value of collaboration and inclusive leadership in creating a harmonious and thriving work environment.

Ethical Use of Power

Leaders who harness their power ethically are able to inspire and empower their teams to achieve greatness.

When leaders use their power in an ethical manner, they create an environment of trust and respect, where employees feel valued and motivated.

Ethical leaders understand the importance of fairness and transparency in decision-making, and they prioritize the well-being of their team members over personal gain.

By setting a positive example and treating others with integrity, ethical leaders foster a culture of accountability and collaboration.

They understand that their power comes with a responsibility to use it for the greater good, and they strive to make decisions that align with their values and the best interests of their team.

In doing so, they not only gain the loyalty and support of their employees, but they also create an atmosphere that encourages innovation and growth.

Ultimately, ethical use of power allows leaders to unlock the true potential of their teams and achieve extraordinary results.

Empowering Others

Now that you've understood the importance of ethical use of power, it's time to delve into the next crucial aspect of effective leadership - empowering others.

As a leader, your true power lies not in your authority, but in your ability to empower and uplift those around you. When you empower others, you create a culture of trust, collaboration, and growth within your team or organization.

By giving your team members the autonomy to make decisions, encouraging their ideas and contributions, and providing them with the necessary resources and support, you enable them to reach their full potential.

Empowering others not only benefits them individually but also leads to collective success and achievement of organizational goals. So, embrace the power of empowering others and witness the remarkable transformation it brings to your leadership journey.

Shifting from Power Over to Power With

By shifting from a position of control to a collaborative approach, you can create a dynamic environment where power is shared and collective decision-making becomes the driving force. Power over others may give a sense of authority, but it often leads to resistance and disengagement.

When you shift to power with others, you empower them to contribute their unique perspectives and skills, fostering a sense of ownership and commitment. This collaborative approach allows for more innovative solutions, as diverse ideas are brought to the table and collective intelligence is harnessed.

Additionally, by involving others in the decision-making process, you build trust and create a culture of mutual respect. This not only enhances teamwork but also boosts morale and motivation.

Shifting from power over to power with is not about giving up control, but rather about leveraging the strengths of your team and creating an environment where everyone feels valued and heard.

Chapter 23: Cultivating Future Leaders

In Chapter 23, you'll explore the importance of cultivating future leaders by focusing on three key points.

First, you'll learn about the significance of identifying potential leaders within your organization and how to spot individuals with leadership potential.

Next, you'll delve into the process of nurturing leadership skill development, providing practical strategies to help these potential leaders thrive.

Lastly, you'll discover the value of implementing succession planning to ensure a smooth transition of leadership and maintain organizational stability.

Identifying Potential Leaders

When it comes to identifying potential leaders, it's important to assess their leadership traits. This involves observing them in action and recognizing their initiative.

By assessing their leadership traits, you can determine if they possess qualities such as confidence, communication skills, and the ability to inspire others.

Observing leaders in action allows you to see how they handle challenges, make decisions, and motivate their team.

Finally, recognizing initiative is crucial. It shows that someone is proactive, takes responsibility, and is willing to go above and beyond.

Assessing Leadership Traits

Unleash your true power as a leader by delving into the depths of your leadership traits, like a deep-sea diver exploring the hidden treasures of the ocean.

Assessing your leadership traits is crucial in understanding your strengths and areas for improvement. Begin by identifying the traits that are essential for effective leadership, such as communication skills, adaptability, empathy, and resilience.

Reflect on your past experiences to gain insights into how these traits have influenced your leadership style. Take note of your successes and challenges, and use them as learning opportunities. Seek feedback from colleagues, mentors, and team members to gain a different perspective on your leadership traits.

Embrace feedback, both positive and constructive, as it will provide valuable insights into areas you can further develop. Additionally, consider taking assessments or participating in leadership development programs to gain a deeper understanding of your leadership traits.

By assessing your leadership traits, you can unlock your true potential as a leader and inspire those around you to do the same.

Observing Leaders in Action

Watch leaders in action to gain valuable insights and see how they inspire and motivate their teams. By observing leaders in action, you can learn firsthand about their communication style, decision-making process, and ability to handle challenges.

Pay attention to how they interact with their team members, how they delegate tasks, and how they provide feedback. Observe their body language, tone of voice, and facial expressions to gain a deeper understanding of their leadership presence.

Look for moments when they inspire their team members through their words and actions, and take note of the strategies they use to motivate their team to achieve their goals.

By closely observing leaders in action, you can gain practical knowledge and inspiration to enhance your own leadership skills and become a more effective leader.

Recognizing Initiative

Take notice of the initiative taken by leaders and see how they inspire their teams, as this can provide valuable insights for your own leadership journey.

Leaders who recognize the importance of initiative understand that it's not enough to simply have a vision and delegate tasks. They actively seek out opportunities to encourage and empower their team members to take ownership of their work and make meaningful contributions.

By recognizing and rewarding initiative, leaders create a culture of innovation and motivation, where individuals feel valued and empowered to take risks and think outside the box. This approach not only fosters creativity and productivity but also builds trust and loyalty within the team.

So, take the time to observe and learn from leaders who excel at recognizing initiative, and incorporate these practices into your own leadership style to unleash the true power of your team.

Nurturing Leadership Skill Development

If you want to nurture leadership skill development, there are three key points to consider.

First, mentoring and coaching can provide valuable guidance and support to aspiring leaders.

Second, providing opportunities for growth, such as challenging projects or additional training, can help develop leadership skills.

Lastly, encouraging networking and collaboration can foster connections and learning from others in the field.

By focusing on these areas, you can help individuals develop their leadership potential and excel in their roles.

Mentoring and Coaching

Improve your leadership skills by harnessing the true power of mentoring and coaching.

Mentoring and coaching are essential tools for personal and professional growth. When you have a mentor or coach, you have someone who can provide guidance, support, and feedback. They can help you identify your strengths and weaknesses, set goals, and develop strategies to achieve them.

A mentor or coach can also challenge you to step out of your comfort zone and push yourself to new heights. They can provide valuable insights and perspectives that you may not have considered before. Through regular meetings and discussions, they can help you navigate through challenges and make sound decisions.

Mentoring and coaching are not just about acquiring new skills and knowledge, but also about building confidence, resilience, and self-awareness. By working with a mentor or coach, you can unlock your full potential and become a more effective and influential leader.

So don't underestimate the power of mentoring and coaching - embrace it and watch your leadership skills soar.

Providing Opportunities for Growth

Embrace the potential for growth by creating opportunities that challenge and inspire you to reach new heights in your leadership journey. Providing opportunities for growth isn't just about offering training programs or promotions; it's about creating an environment that fosters continuous learning and development.

Seek out projects or assignments that push you outside of your comfort zone and require you to stretch your skills and abilities. Surround yourself with a diverse group of people who can offer different perspectives and insights, and be open to feedback and constructive criticism.

Take the initiative to seek out new experiences and take on new responsibilities. By actively seeking opportunities for growth, you won't only expand your own capabilities but also inspire those around you to do the same. Remember, true leadership isn't about holding onto power but about unleashing it in others.

Encouraging Networking and Collaboration

Take the time to connect and collaborate with others, as networking can ignite a spark of inspiration and create powerful relationships that will propel you forward in your leadership journey.

By actively seeking out opportunities to connect with people in your field, you open yourself up to a wealth of knowledge and experiences that can broaden your perspective and enhance your leadership skills.

Collaboration, on the other hand, allows you to tap into the collective intelligence and creativity of a group, leading to innovative solutions and better decision-making.

Whether it's attending industry conferences, joining professional organizations, or simply reaching out to colleagues for a coffee chat, networking and collaboration are essential tools for any leader looking to expand their influence and make a meaningful impact.

So, don't underestimate the power of building connections and working together with others – it can be the key to unlocking your true leadership potential.

Implementing Succession Planning

Are you looking to ensure the long-term success of your organization by developing a strong pipeline of future leaders?

In this discussion, we'll explore the key points of establishing a succession planning process, developing and preparing successors, and managing the transition.

By implementing a well-defined succession planning process, you can identify and groom future leaders, ensuring a smooth transition when key positions become vacant.

Developing and preparing successors involves providing them with the necessary training, mentoring, and opportunities to develop their skills and knowledge.

Finally, effective transition management is crucial for ensuring a seamless handover of responsibilities and maintaining continuity in leadership.

Establishing the Succession Planning Process

Establishing the succession planning process is like laying the foundation for a thriving leadership legacy, where each brick represents a future leader ready to take the helm. It's a crucial step in ensuring the long-term success and sustainability of an organization.

By implementing a robust succession planning process, you can identify and develop the next generation of leaders, ensuring a seamless transition when the time comes. This process involves identifying key positions within the organization and potential candidates who have the skills, knowledge, and potential to step into these roles.

It also involves providing them with the necessary training, mentoring, and development opportunities to prepare them for future leadership positions. Additionally, it's essential to create a culture that values and encourages leadership development, where employees see a clear path to advancement and are motivated to develop their skills and capabilities.

By establishing a well-defined succession planning process, you can create a pipeline of talent, reduce the risk of leadership gaps, and unleash the true power of leadership within your organization.

Developing and Preparing Successors

Developing and preparing successors is a vital step in ensuring a smooth transition of leadership, where future leaders are equipped with the necessary skills and support to take on key roles within the organization.

By investing time and resources into the development of potential successors, organizations can cultivate a pool of talented individuals who are ready to step into leadership positions when the time comes.

This process involves identifying high-potential individuals, assessing their strengths and areas for development, and providing them with targeted training and mentoring opportunities.

It is essential to provide successors with exposure to different aspects of the business, allowing them to gain a comprehensive understanding of the organization and its challenges.

Additionally, providing them with opportunities to lead projects or teams can help build their confidence and hone their leadership skills.

Succession planning should also include regular performance evaluations and feedback sessions to ensure that successors are progressing and addressing any development needs.

By taking a proactive approach to developing and preparing successors, organizations can not only ensure a smooth transition of leadership but also foster a culture of continuous learning and growth.

Transition Management

During the transition management process, you must navigate the delicate balance between preserving the legacy of your predecessor and paving the way for a new era of growth and innovation.

It is a critical time when the organization looks to you for guidance and direction.

To successfully manage this transition, you need to understand the strengths and weaknesses of your team and align their skills with the upcoming challenges.

Communicate openly and transparently with your team, addressing any concerns or uncertainties they may have.

Encourage them to embrace change and empower them to contribute their ideas and expertise.

As a leader, you must also ensure a smooth handover of responsibilities, providing clear expectations and support to your successor.

By managing the transition effectively, you can build trust, inspire confidence, and set the stage for a successful leadership journey.

Chapter 24: Leadership Evaluation and Development

In this chapter, you'll explore the importance of leadership evaluation and development. You'll learn why it's crucial to regularly assess the effectiveness of leaders within your organization and identify areas for improvement.

Additionally, you'll discover various methods for evaluating leadership skills and qualities, as well as effective strategies for implementing leadership development programs that can empower your future leaders.

The Need for Leadership Evaluation

If you want to truly unleash the power of leadership, it's essential to evaluate performance. This involves providing constructive feedback and setting clear goals. By assessing performance, you can identify areas of strength and opportunities for improvement. This allows leaders to grow and develop. Constructive feedback helps leaders understand their impact on others and make necessary adjustments. Goal setting provides a clear direction for growth and achievement.

Performance Assessment

By properly utilizing performance assessment techniques, you can tap into your team's full potential and unlock their true capabilities.

Performance assessment allows you to evaluate each individual's strengths and weaknesses, identify areas for improvement, and provide targeted feedback and coaching.

This process not only helps you understand your team members' current performance levels, but also enables you to set clear expectations and goals for their development.

By regularly assessing performance, you can track progress, address any issues or roadblocks, and ensure that everyone is aligned towards achieving the team's objectives.

Moreover, performance assessment provides an opportunity for recognition and rewards, which can boost motivation and morale within your team.

By giving your team members the feedback and support they need, you can empower them to reach their full potential and contribute to the success of your organization.

Constructive Feedback

Imagine a feedback session as a sculptor molding a masterpiece, carefully shaping and refining your team members' skills and abilities to create a collective work of art.

Constructive feedback is an essential tool for effective leadership, as it helps individuals grow and develop their potential. When giving feedback, it's important to be specific and focus on behavior rather than personal traits. By highlighting areas for improvement and offering suggestions for growth, you can empower your team members to reach their full potential.

Additionally, it's crucial to create a safe and supportive environment where individuals feel comfortable receiving feedback and are open to making necessary changes. Remember, constructive feedback isn't about criticizing or tearing down, but about building up and inspiring positive change.

By providing feedback that's insightful, informative, and practical, you can unleash the true power of leadership and foster a culture of continuous improvement within your team.

Goal Setting

Setting clear and achievable goals is the key to unlocking your team's potential and driving them towards success. As a leader, it's crucial to provide your team with a clear direction and purpose.

By setting specific and measurable goals, you enable your team members to focus their efforts and align their actions with the desired outcomes. Clear goals not only provide clarity but also serve as a motivation for your team, as they can see the progress they're making towards achieving them.

It's important to ensure that these goals are attainable, as setting unrealistic expectations can lead to demotivation and a sense of failure. Break down larger goals into smaller, manageable milestones, allowing your team to celebrate small wins along the way.

Additionally, involve your team in the goal-setting process, fostering a sense of ownership and commitment.

Regularly review and adjust goals as needed, ensuring they remain relevant and challenging. By setting clear and achievable goals, you empower your team to unleash their true potential and drive them towards success.

Methods for Leadership Evaluation

In this discussion, you'll explore three key methods for leadership evaluation: 360-Degree Feedback, Leadership Assessment Tools, and Individual Development Plans. These methods are designed to provide a comprehensive assessment of a leader's strengths and areas for improvement. This allows for a well-rounded evaluation. By utilizing these tools, you'll gain valuable insights into your leadership skills and be able to create a personalized plan for growth and development.

360-Degree Feedback

Unlock the true power of leadership with 360-degree feedback, a transformative tool that reveals hidden strengths and weaknesses through multiple perspectives.

By incorporating feedback from various sources including peers, subordinates, and superiors, leaders gain a holistic view of their performance and impact. This feedback mechanism enables leaders to identify blind spots, improve self-awareness, and make informed decisions about their leadership style and approach.

Through the collection of diverse feedback, leaders gain valuable insights and can develop targeted strategies for growth and development. They can build on their strengths and address areas for improvement, ultimately enhancing their effectiveness as leaders.

Moreover, 360-degree feedback fosters a culture of open communication and trust, as it encourages individuals to provide honest and constructive feedback. By embracing this tool, leaders can unlock their true potential and drive meaningful change within their organizations.

Leadership Assessment Tools

Leaders can leverage leadership assessment tools to gain valuable insights into their strengths and areas for improvement, enabling them to make informed decisions about their leadership approach and drive meaningful change within their organizations.

These tools provide leaders with a comprehensive evaluation of their leadership style, skills, and behaviors, allowing them to identify areas where they excel and areas where they may need to focus on development.

By understanding their own strengths and weaknesses, leaders can tailor their leadership approach to better meet the needs of their team and organization.

Furthermore, leadership assessment tools can also help leaders identify blind spots and biases that may be hindering their effectiveness.

Armed with this knowledge, leaders can take steps to address these areas and enhance their leadership capabilities.

Overall, leadership assessment tools offer a practical and insightful way for leaders to gain self-awareness, improve their leadership skills, and drive positive change within their organizations.

Individual Development Plans

Improve your leadership skills and drive personal growth with individual development plans. These plans are essential tools that allow you to identify your strengths, weaknesses, and areas for improvement. By setting specific and measurable goals, you can create a roadmap for your professional development.

Individual development plans provide a structured approach to enhance your leadership abilities by focusing on areas such as communication, decision-making, and problem-solving. They encourage self-reflection, enabling you to gain a deeper understanding of your leadership style and how it impacts others.

Additionally, these plans provide opportunities for you to seek out new experiences and challenges that'll further develop your skills. With an individual development plan, you can take control of your own growth and unlock your true potential as a leader.

Effective Leadership Development Programs

In order to develop effective leaders, it's crucial to understand the elements of a good leadership development program. This includes providing opportunities for skill-building, fostering mentorship relationships, and encouraging self-reflection.

Implementing such programs requires clear goals, dedicated resources, and a supportive organizational culture.

Measuring the effectiveness of leadership development programs is essential to ensure that they're delivering the desired outcomes and making a positive impact on the organization. This can be done through feedback mechanisms, performance evaluations, and tracking the progress of program participants.

Elements of a Good Program

Picture yourself as a captain at the helm of a ship, navigating through uncharted seas towards a prosperous destination - that's the essence of a good leadership program. A good program should provide you with the necessary tools and skills to navigate the challenges and uncertainties that come with leading others.

It should offer a comprehensive curriculum that covers various aspects of leadership, from communication and decision-making to problem-solving and team building. A good program will also prioritize experiential learning, giving you opportunities to apply what you've learned in real-life scenarios. It should challenge you to step out of your comfort zone, push your limits, and discover your true potential as a leader.

Additionally, a good leadership program should provide ongoing support and feedback, helping you to continuously improve and grow. It should foster a collaborative and supportive environment where you can learn from others and build meaningful connections. Ultimately, a good program should empower you to become a leader who not only achieves results but also inspires and influences others to reach their full potential.

Implementing Development Programs

Enrich your leadership skills by implementing development programs that provide you with the necessary tools and resources to excel in your role.

These programs offer a unique opportunity to enhance your abilities, broaden your knowledge, and develop new strategies for success.

By participating in these programs, you can gain valuable insights from industry experts, learn from real-life case studies, and engage in interactive workshops that challenge your thinking and expand your perspective.

Additionally, these programs often provide access to a network of like-minded individuals who can support and inspire your growth as a leader.

Through hands-on experiences and practical exercises, you can apply the concepts learned in these programs directly to your own work, allowing you to see immediate results and make a positive impact on your team and organization.

So, take the initiative and invest in your development by enrolling in a development program today.

It's a powerful step towards unlocking your true leadership potential.

Measuring Effectiveness

Improve your leadership skills by gauging the impact of your development programs through effective measurement techniques, giving you a clear view of your progress and igniting a fire within you to strive for even greater success.

Measuring the effectiveness of your development programs is crucial in order to understand whether they're actually achieving their intended outcomes. By using measurement techniques such as surveys, feedback sessions, and performance evaluations, you can gather valuable data that'll help you assess the effectiveness of your programs.

This data will provide you with insights into what's working well and what areas need improvement. It'll also help you identify any gaps or areas of opportunity that you may not have been aware of. Armed with this information, you can make informed decisions on how to adjust and refine your development programs to ensure that they're truly making a difference.

So, take the time to measure the impact of your efforts and use this knowledge to continuously improve your leadership skills and achieve even greater success.

Chapter 25: Reflecting on Leadership Styles and Lessons

In this chapter, you'll explore the importance of comparing different leadership styles and how they impact the effectiveness of a leader.

By examining notable leaders and their unique leadership styles, you'll gain insight into what works and what doesn't in various situations.

Finally, you'll reflect on the key lessons learned throughout this book and draw your own conclusions about the essential qualities and approaches of successful leaders.

Comparing Leadership Styles

When considering leadership styles, it's important to explore the Leadership Style Matrix. This matrix categorizes different leadership approaches based on their level of authority and influence. Each style has its own set of strengths and weaknesses. It's crucial to take these into account when determining the most effective approach for a given situation. Understanding the appropriate contexts for each style will enable you to unleash the true power of leadership. By adapting your approach to suit the needs and dynamics of your team.

Leadership Style Matrix

Unleash the true power of your leadership by exploring the Leadership Style Matrix. This matrix provides a comprehensive framework for understanding and evaluating different leadership styles.

By examining the four quadrants of the matrix - autocratic, democratic, laissez-faire, and transformational - you can gain valuable insights into your own leadership approach and identify areas for growth.

The autocratic style, characterized by a top-down approach, can be effective in situations that require quick decision-making and strong direction. On the other hand, the democratic style promotes collaboration and empowers team members to contribute their ideas and opinions.

The laissez-faire style gives individuals the freedom to take ownership of their work and encourages creativity. Lastly, the transformational style inspires and motivates others to achieve their full potential by setting high expectations and providing support.

By understanding the strengths and weaknesses of each style, you can adapt your leadership approach to different situations and unleash your true leadership potential.

Strengths and Weaknesses of Each Style

Explore the Leadership Style Matrix to uncover the strengths and weaknesses of each leadership style, helping you enhance your leadership skills and create a more enjoyable and effective work environment.

Understanding the strengths and weaknesses of each style is crucial in developing your leadership abilities. For example, the authoritarian style may provide clear direction and quick decision-making, but it can also stifle creativity and collaboration.

On the other hand, the democratic style encourages participation and innovation, but it may lead to slower decision-making and a lack of accountability.

The laissez-faire style promotes autonomy and creativity, but it can also result in a lack of direction and control.

By recognizing these strengths and weaknesses, you can adapt your leadership approach to suit different situations, maximize your strengths, and mitigate your weaknesses.

This knowledge empowers you to become a more effective leader, fostering a positive and productive work environment for your team.

Appropriate Contexts for Each Style

To truly harness the power of your leadership style, it's crucial to understand the appropriate contexts for each style - knowing when to be authoritative, democratic, or laissez-faire can make all the difference in creating an extraordinary work environment where your team can thrive beyond imagination.

In the appropriate context, an authoritative leadership style can be highly effective when quick decisions need to be made, or in situations where there's a clear hierarchy and chain of command. This style works best when the leader has expert knowledge and experience, and when the team members are less experienced or require guidance.

On the other hand, a democratic leadership style is most suitable when collaboration and input from team members are crucial. This style fosters a sense of ownership and empowerment among team members, leading to increased motivation and creativity.

Finally, a laissez-faire leadership style can be effective in situations where team members are highly skilled and motivated, and when they require minimal supervision. This style allows for autonomy and freedom, enabling team members to take ownership of their work and explore innovative solutions.

Understanding the appropriate context for each style will enable you to adapt your leadership approach and create a work environment that maximizes the potential of your team.

Notable Leaders and Their Leadership Styles

When analyzing the journeys of notable leaders and their leadership styles, it's important to consider the impact they've had on their respective fields. By examining their approaches to leadership, we can gain valuable insights and learn important lessons that can be applied to our own leadership roles.

These leaders serve as powerful examples of how effective leadership can make a significant difference, inspiring us to strive for greatness in our own endeavors.

Analyzing their Journeys

From humble beginnings to remarkable achievements, their journeys captivate and inspire.

It is fascinating to analyze how these notable leaders navigated through challenges and setbacks to reach their goals.

Their stories teach us valuable lessons about perseverance, resilience, and the importance of staying true to oneself.

By studying their journeys, we can gain insights into their leadership styles and understand the strategies they used to overcome obstacles.

These leaders not only had a clear vision but also possessed the ability to inspire and motivate others to join them on their path to success.

Their journeys remind us that leadership isn't just about authority, but about unleashing the true power within oneself and others.

Impact of their Leadership

Their leadership left a lasting impact, inspiring others to achieve greatness and setting a precedent for future generations. By harnessing their influence beyond traditional authority, these leaders were able to create a ripple effect that extended far beyond their immediate sphere of control.

Their ability to motivate and empower others resulted in increased collaboration, innovation, and productivity within their organizations. Through their visionary and inclusive leadership styles, they created a culture of trust and transparency, where individuals felt valued and motivated to contribute their best.

This impact was not limited to their immediate teams, but also spread to the wider community, as they actively sought opportunities to give back and make a positive difference. Their leadership legacy continues to inspire and guide aspiring leaders to think beyond the confines of authority, recognizing that the true power lies in their ability to influence and inspire others.

Lessons to Learn

One key lesson to learn is that leaders can have a lasting impact by inspiring and empowering others, despite any potential objections to their methods.

When leaders go beyond their authority and tap into their true power, they become catalysts for change and transformation.

They understand that true leadership is not about exerting control or dominance, but about creating an environment where everyone feels valued and empowered to contribute their best.

By embodying the qualities of authenticity, empathy, and vulnerability, leaders can connect with their teams on a deeper level and inspire them to reach their full potential.

They recognize that leadership is not a one-size-fits-all approach and are willing to adapt their style to meet the unique needs and strengths of their team members.

They foster a culture of collaboration and innovation, encouraging diverse perspectives and fostering an environment where everyone feels safe to share their ideas and take risks.

Ultimately, these leaders leave a lasting legacy by creating a positive and inclusive work culture that not only drives results but also nurtures the personal and professional growth of their team members.

Concluding Thoughts on Leadership

The future of leadership is constantly evolving, as new challenges and opportunities arise.

In order to thrive in this ever-changing landscape, it's crucial to invest in your personal leadership development.

By continuously honing your skills, adapting to new technologies, and staying ahead of trends, you can build sustainable leadership practices.

These practices will lead to long-term success.

Future of Leadership

In envisioning the future of leadership, it's crucial to harness the true potential and unleash the power that lies within each individual.

The traditional hierarchical model of leadership, where authority is centralized and top-down, is no longer sufficient in today's rapidly changing world.

The future of leadership lies in recognizing that leadership is not limited to a select few, but can be found in every individual within an organization.

By empowering individuals to take ownership of their work, fostering a culture of collaboration and innovation, and providing opportunities for personal and professional growth, leaders can tap into the collective intelligence and creativity of their teams.

This approach to leadership not only produces better results but also cultivates a sense of purpose and fulfillment among team members.

The future of leadership is about creating an environment where everyone can contribute their unique skills and perspectives, and where leadership is a shared responsibility.

As technology continues to advance and global challenges become more complex, organizations need leaders who can adapt, inspire, and bring out the best in others.

By embracing this future-oriented approach to leadership, we can unlock the true power of individuals and unleash their potential to drive meaningful change.

Personal Leadership Development

Imagine a future where individuals are empowered to cultivate their own personal leadership skills and develop into the best versions of themselves.

In this future, personal leadership development is not limited to a select few, but is accessible to everyone. It is a journey of self-discovery and growth, where individuals are encouraged to reflect on their strengths and weaknesses, and take proactive steps to enhance their leadership abilities.

Through various tools and techniques, individuals are able to develop their emotional intelligence, communication skills, and decision-making abilities. They're empowered to set goals, take risks, and learn from their failures.

Personal leadership development also emphasizes the importance of self-care and well-being, as individuals understand that their own growth and development is intrinsically linked to their ability to lead effectively.

It is a continuous process, where individuals are constantly learning, adapting, and evolving. In this future, personal leadership development is not just a nice-to-have, but a necessity for individuals to thrive in their personal and professional lives.

It's a transformative journey that enables individuals to unleash their true potential and make a positive impact in the world.

So, imagine a future where personal leadership development isn't just a buzzword, but a reality that empowers individuals to become the best leaders they can be.

Building Sustainable Leadership Practices

Now that you've gained a deeper understanding of personal leadership development, it's time to explore the next step in unleashing your true power as a leader: building sustainable leadership practices.

Building sustainable leadership practices involves creating systems and processes that not only support your personal growth, but also empower those around you to become leaders themselves.

It's about fostering a culture of continuous learning and development, where everyone is encouraged to take ownership of their own leadership journeys.

By implementing sustainable leadership practices, you can create a ripple effect that extends far beyond your immediate sphere of influence, making a lasting impact on your organization and the world.

So, let's dive into the strategies and techniques that'll enable you to build sustainable leadership practices and unlock the full potential of your leadership abilities.

Don't miss out!

Visit the website below and you can sign up to receive emails whenever Adam Poliman publishes a new book. There's no charge and no obligation.

https://books2read.com/r/B-A-VSRY-DCHNC

BOOKS 2 READ

Connecting independent readers to independent writers.

Did you love *Beyond Authority- Unleashing The True Power Of Leadership*? Then you should read *The Emotion Code: Decoding Emotional Intelligence*[1] by Adam Poliman!

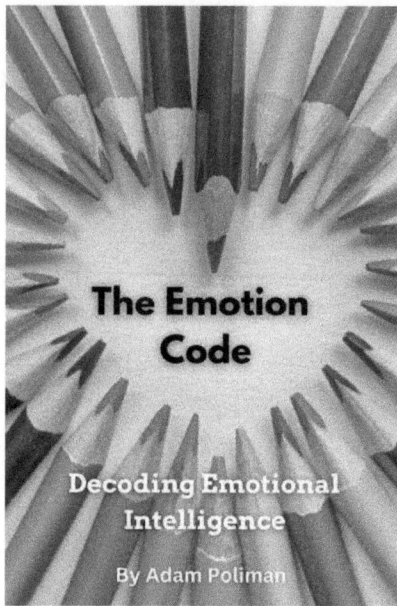

"The Emotion Code: Decoding Emotional Intelligence"

In a world driven by logic and reason, the profound impact of emotions often remains hidden in plain sight. Emotions are the essence of our human experience, shaping our thoughts, actions, and relationships. Yet, for many, they are a mysterious labyrinth that can be difficult to navigate. This is where "The Emotion Code: Decoding Emotional Intelligence" steps in, offering a transformative journey into the heart of emotional intelligence.

This groundbreaking book delves deep into the intricate web of human emotions, unraveling their intricate codes to unlock the power

---

of emotional intelligence. Drawing on the latest insights from psychology, neuroscience, and personal development, it provides a comprehensive guide to understanding, harnessing, and mastering your emotions.

Author [Author Name], a renowned expert in the field of emotional intelligence, takes you on a compelling exploration of your inner world. Through relatable stories, scientific research, and practical exercises, you'll discover:

The Language of Emotions: Learn to decipher the nuanced language of your feelings and gain insights into what your emotions are trying to tell you.

Emotional Resilience: Develop the tools and techniques to build emotional resilience, allowing you to navigate life's challenges with grace and strength.

Relationship Mastery: Explore how emotions impact your relationships, and acquire skills to enhance your communication, empathy, and connection with others.

Self-Awareness: Dive deep into self-awareness, uncovering your unique emotional patterns and triggers, and discovering the profound influence they have on your life choices.

Emotional Healing: Discover strategies to release past emotional baggage, freeing yourself from the burdens that may be holding you back from a fulfilling life.

Personal Growth: Harness the power of your emotions to fuel personal growth and transformation, creating a life aligned with your true desires and values.

"The Emotion Code" is not just a book; it's a roadmap to a more emotionally intelligent life. Whether you're seeking to enhance your career, strengthen your relationships, or simply achieve a greater sense of well-being, this book offers the guidance and tools you need to thrive.

It's time to decode the enigma of your emotions and harness their incredible potential. "The Emotion Code: Decoding Emotional

Intelligence" is your key to unlocking a more joyful, meaningful, and emotionally fulfilling life. Dive into this transformative journey today and embark on a path to emotional mastery that will serve you for a lifetime.

Read more at https://optimizationtime.com.

Also by Adam Poliman

Watch for more at https://optimizationtime.com.

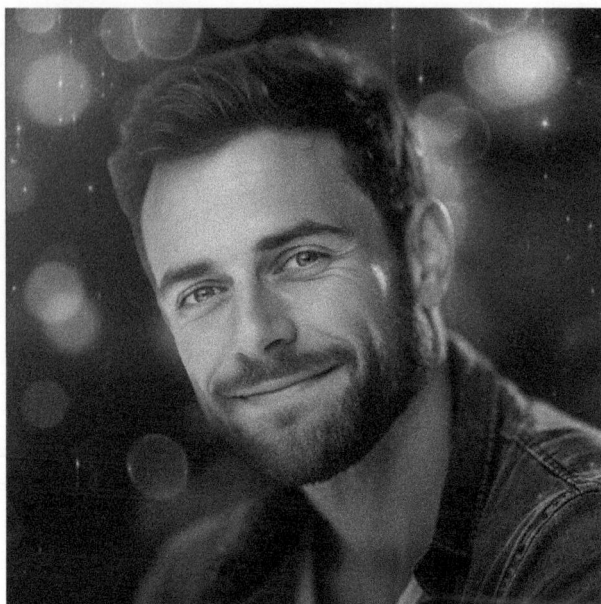

About the Author

Adam Poliman is a renowned author in the personal improvement space, dedicated to helping individuals unlock their full potential and lead fulfilling lives. With a passion for personal growth and a deep understanding of human psychology, Adam combines his expertise with practical insights to empower readers to make positive changes. His thought-provoking books offer actionable strategies and transformative techniques that inspire readers to overcome challenges, cultivate resilience, and achieve their goals. Through his writing, Adam seeks to guide readers on a transformative journey of self-discovery, encouraging them to embrace personal development and create a life of purpose and fulfillment.

Read more at https://optimizationtime.com.

Milton Keynes UK
Ingram Content Group UK Ltd.
UKHW040904100923
428413UK00001B/11

9 798215 971086